"Working with *The Better Boundaries Workbook* is like having personal sessions with a very wise and compassionate therapist. You will learn actionable ways to stand up for yourself and make your needs clear so all your relationships can thrive. The exercises and insights this helpful guide offers will let you tap into your most empowered and authentic self."

—**Jennifer King Lindley**, award-winning health journalist, and author of *Find Your Joy*

"In *The Better Boundaries Workbook*, Sharon Martin discusses a tremendously useful topic that most people have difficulty understanding, and even therapists struggle to describe: boundaries. She not only explains, in clear terms, exactly what boundaries are, she also walks you through the process of building yours. Ever wondered whether your boundaries need improvement, how healthy boundaries look, or how to create and strengthen them? You'll find all the answers here."

—**Jonice Webb, PhD**, bestselling author of *Running on Empty* and *Running on Empty No More*

"This workbook does an excellent job of explaining the layers of boundaries. *The Better Boundaries Workbook* is an easy-to-follow how-to guide for self-improvement. What I loved most about the book is the simple explanation of what boundaries are, how boundaries impact our well-being, and simple tools to increase and protect boundaries. Sharon Martin has produced a well-written book that is instrumental in self-empowerment and mental health."

—**Natalie Jones, PsyD, LPCC**, owner of Lifetime Counseling and Consulting®, creator of the *A Date With Darkness Podcast*®, expert witness, and media therapist

"*The Better Boundaries Workbook* is a clear, caring guide to help people build stronger boundaries. Sharon Martin has done it again with this brilliant workbook, a powerful tool for anyone looking to not be taken advantage of. When you are ready to 'do the work,' this workbook gives you thoughtful exercises to look within your own patterns, and teaches you how to create new programming that better serves you. I love this book, and it will forever be in my referral library to help those with boundary challenges."

—**Tracy A. Malone**, founder of Narcissist Abuse Support

"Boundaries can easily bring up feelings of guilt, fear, or anxiety, but Sharon makes the difficult process of setting limits feel accessible. Learn why boundaries are important, and how to overcome the emotional difficulties of honoring your needs. With the many scripts, vignettes, and other tools in this guide, you'll discover a step-by-step process for maintaining boundaries in every area of your life. This workbook is a must-read for anyone struggling with people-pleasing, perfectionism, or codependency."

—**April Snow, LMFT**, licensed psychotherapist, and author of
Mindfulness Workbook for Stress Relief

"Once again, with *The Better Boundaries Workbook*, Sharon Martin shares her insight and her expertise in her down-to-earth style. Martin's work is clear, practical, and easy to relate to. The chapters for setting boundaries, communicating needs, and working with boundary violations are well laid out, and have actionable steps throughout. I'm excited to use *The Better Boundaries Workbook* with my therapy and coaching clients for years to come!"

—**Elizabeth Cush, LCPC**, licensed clinical professional counselor, life coach, and
host of the *Awaken Your Wise Woman* podcast

"*The Better Boundaries Workbook* is the most comprehensive resource available to help people struggling with setting healthy boundaries, people-pleasing, and assertive communication. Sharon Martin expertly guides the reader to create a clear and personalized action plan."

—**Marni Feuerman, MSW, PsyD**, psychotherapist, and author of
Ghosted and Breadcrumbed

THE BETTER

Boundaries

WORKBOOK

A CBT-BASED PROGRAM *to*

HELP YOU SET LIMITS, EXPRESS YOUR NEEDS,

and **CREATE HEALTHY RELATIONSHIPS**

SHARON MARTIN, MSW, LCSW

New Harbinger Publications, Inc.

Publisher's Note

The four steps to setting boundaries in chapter 4 are adapted with permission from MOVING BEYOND BETRAYAL by Vicki Tidwell Palmer, copyright © 2016 Vicki Tidwell Palmer. Used by permission of Central Recovery Press.

Distributed in Canada by Raincoast Books

NEW HARBINGER PUBLICATIONS is a registered trademark of New Harbinger Publications, Inc.

Cover design by Amy Daniel

Acquired by Ryan Buresh

Edited by Karen Levy

Library of Congress Cataloging-in-Publication Data on file

Printed in the United States of America

24   23   22

10   9   8   7   6   5   4   3

Contents

Part Four: Practicing Boundary Skills with Yourself

Introduction

Welcome to *The Better Boundaries Workbook*.

I'm excited to share this book with you because I know, from personal and professional experience, that healthy boundaries can transform your life. If you struggle to stand up for yourself, ask for what you need, or feel guilty or afraid when you do, learning to set boundaries can increase your self-esteem and confidence, and help you create respectful, satisfying relationships. Of course, this doesn't happen all at once. As you know, setting boundaries is tough. However, I'm confident that with the concepts in this book and committed practice, you can learn to set effective boundaries.

About This Workbook

Through my work as a psychotherapist, it became clear that so many of my clients' struggles were related to their difficulty setting boundaries—and there was a need for an evidence-based guide to teach these skills. And, so, I wrote this workbook to share the practical skills and strategies for setting boundaries that I've successfully used with my clients.

In part one of this workbook, you'll learn what boundaries are, why we need them, and why they're hard to set. Part two focuses on how to create and communicate boundaries, and how to handle boundary violations. In part three, you'll learn boundary skills with others, including at work; with your partner, children, extended family, and friends; and with difficult people. And in part four, you'll practice boundary skills with yourself, including respecting other people's boundaries and creating healthy limits and habits for yourself.

This workbook uses cognitive behavioral therapy (CBT), an evidence-based approach to understanding the connection between our thoughts, feelings, and behaviors. The CBT exercises in this book will help you identify inaccurate thoughts and beliefs that are making it difficult for you to set boundaries and replace them with thoughts that are more accurate and helpful.

In addition to CBT, I use mindfulness and self-compassion concepts. By tuning in to the present, mindfulness can help you regulate your emotions, especially when you're overwhelmed or upset. And self-compassion fosters self-acceptance, resiliency, and motivation.

How to Use This Workbook

The concepts and exercises in this book build upon each other, so I recommend reading from start to finish. Some chapters may not seem relevant to you, but I encourage you to still read them, as you'll probably find useful tips for setting boundaries in every chapter.

Learning new skills takes a lot of practice. One of the biggest problems people have when trying to change is they give up too soon—before they've practiced new thoughts, feelings, and behaviors enough for them to feel comfortable and be effective. For this reason, I've provided a variety of tools and ways to access them.

Written Exercises

This workbook is full of exercises and reflective questions designed to help you practice and integrate the concepts you're learning. Some can be done as you're reading; others will require more thought or ask you to complete them over a week or so. Try your best to do them all.

Online Materials

To make it easier for you to repeat the exercises in this book, some are available electronically at http://www.newharbinger.com/47582. Please print additional copies and repeat them as often as it's helpful.

Journal

You may also find it helpful to use a journal or notebook to capture your thoughts, feelings, struggles, and successes. This will reinforce what you're learning and help you overcome barriers and track your progress.

Therapy

Some difficult feelings may come up as you complete this workbook, and a therapist can help you process them and troubleshoot more complex boundary issues. If you experience increased symptoms of depression, anxiety, or suicidal thoughts, please consult a mental health or medical professional immediately.

If you are a therapist using this workbook with clients, I have written a guide for you that is available at http://www.newharbinger.com/47582.

Final Thoughts

Setting boundaries is both challenging and rewarding. This workbook can help you overcome the challenges and reap the rewards of better boundaries!

Part One

INTRODUCTION TO BOUNDARIES

Chapter 1

What Are Boundaries and Why Do We Need Them?

Boundaries are essential to our health, happiness, and success. However, setting boundaries is a challenge for many of us. We're not used to standing up for ourselves and asking for what we need. We're afraid to say *no* because we don't want to disappoint or offend people. And we lose track of who we are and what's important to us because we're so focused on what other people want or need. Consequently, we end up frustrated, exhausted, unappreciated, and mistreated. But we can learn to set boundaries with kindness, assertively ask for what we need, and create more satisfying and respectful relationships.

To get started, we'll look at the functions of boundaries, how a lack of boundaries negatively affects us, and the benefits of learning how to set healthy boundaries.

What Are Boundaries?

A boundary is a dividing line that defines who you are as an individual and how you'll interact with others. Boundaries define what's *me* (my body, my feelings, my property, my responsibilities, and so forth) and what's *not me*. Boundaries also communicate how we want to be treated by others, what's okay and not okay with us, and how close we want to get (physically and emotionally) to others.

Boundaries take a variety of forms. For example, physical boundaries protect your space, body, and property. Sexual boundaries protect your right to consent, to ask for what you want sexually, and to receive honesty about your partner's sexual history. Emotional boundaries allow you to have your own thoughts and feelings and protect you from emotional harm such as invalidation or betrayal. Time boundaries help you manage your time, so you don't commit to things you don't want to do or end up overworked.

Boundaries Differentiate You from Me

One of the primary functions of a boundary is to differentiate one thing from another—or in this case, one person from another. Boundaries make it clear that you're a unique, autonomous person, not simply an extension of someone else, such as your parents or spouse. This differentiation is important because it defines your identity and clarifies what you are and are not responsible for.

When you set boundaries, you assert your individuality. We all have our own thoughts, feelings, values, goals, and interests. But sometimes others are threatened or confused by our differences and want us to think, feel, and act as they do. And we, too, may be afraid of being different—assuming it will lead to criticism or rejection—so we hide our true selves, allowing others to tell us who we are. Psychologists use the term "enmeshment" to describe this type of undifferentiation. In enmeshed relationships, there aren't boundaries. Everyone is expected to toe the line, meaning everyone should think, feel, and behave the same. In an enmeshed or boundaryless relationship, you live your life based on what other people want you to do or what they think is right instead of deciding for yourself.

Boundaries create a healthy separation between you and others and define who you are, so you can be yourself and make choices that are right for you.

Boundaries Define Who You Are

A lack of boundaries can leave you unsure of who you are, what you need, what you like to do, what matters to you, and what you believe in. Without boundaries, you lose your true self because there's no separation between you and someone else. Kristin is a perfect example of how we can "lose ourselves" when we don't have boundaries.

Life was going great for Kristin. She was thrilled with her new job teaching art and spent Saturday mornings training for half-marathons with a close group of friends. And on Sunday nights, she volunteered for a teen crisis line, a cause close to her heart following her sister's struggle with depression. However, this all changed when she started dating Nick. Nick was moody and angry, and as their relationship progressed, Kristin's mood suffered too. She spent more and more time trying to make him feel better, helping him find a more fulfilling job, and encouraging him to see a therapist. She gave up volunteering for the crisis line so she could be with Nick, but he usually spent the time tinkering in the garage alone. She also cut back on running with her friends because Nick thought they were "snobby." Instead, they socialized with his friends. Kristen found them immature, but not wanting to anger Nick, she didn't say anything.

Kristin went from a happy, confident woman with a sense of purpose, close friends, and knowing what was important to feeling lonely and discouraged. She gave up her hobbies and friends. She absorbed Nick's moods and problems and they became her own. She didn't know how to hold a boundary between herself and Nick, so she got *swallowed up* by Nick's feelings, needs, and interests.

It's easy to see the difference in Kristin before and after Nick, but when this happens in childhood it's harder to spot because you may not have ever developed a strong sense of identity and purpose.

Boundaries Define What You're Responsible For

In Kristin's story, you saw how she took responsibility for Nick's problems and tried to solve them for him. On one hand, this is a caring thing to do, but ultimately, they aren't problems she can solve. She can provide support and guidance, but she can't get him a more fulfilling job or make him go to therapy. Those things are in Nick's control and are, therefore, his responsibility. Let's look at one more example that highlights how boundaries define what we're responsible for.

Freddy discovered that his wife, Maria, had been texting a male colleague late at night, sharing personal stories and pictures of herself. Freddy thought it was inappropriate and felt hurt and angry. He confronted Maria and her response was, "Why are you making such a big deal about this? You're never home anyway! Maybe if I wasn't so lonely, I wouldn't be texting James!" Maria didn't take responsibility for her actions (texting James) or her feelings (loneliness). Instead, she blamed Freddy and tried to make him responsible for her behavior and feelings. Freddy probably contributed to their marital problems, but he was not responsible for Maria's behavior or feelings, neither of which he can control.

Since boundaries help define us as individuals, they also make clear that we're responsible for our own thoughts, feelings, actions, words, and bodies—but we're not responsible for things we can't control, namely how other people feel and what they do. And as you saw with Freddy and Maria, unclear boundaries can lead to blaming and expecting someone else to solve your problems. When there are healthy, appropriate boundaries, everyone takes responsibility for their own feelings and actions.

Boundaries Are Limits

The second primary function of boundaries is to set limits. Boundaries communicate how you want to be treated, what you need, and what you expect. Limits are necessary because they protect you from being hurt by others.

You also need limits for yourself. Boundaries guide your decisions and behavior and stop you from doing things that aren't in your own best interest, like drinking too much or overspending. Setting limits for yourself also ensures that you focus on what's most important to you and that you spend your time, energy, and money according to your goals and values.

Boundaries Provide Physical and Emotional Safety

Safety is one of our most basic needs. We need to be physically safe from harm and feel emotionally safe to form trusting relationships, feel good about ourselves, solve complex problems, and so on. In the 1940s, psychologist Abraham Maslow created a Hierarchy of Needs that remains a helpful way to conceptualize that humans must first meet their basic needs before they can devote time and energy to more complex and abstract needs, such as feeling appreciated or doing meaningful work. Maslow placed safety at the bottom of the Hierarchy of Needs, second only to our physiological needs (food, water, shelter, sleep).

PHYSICAL SAFETY

Refusing to get into a car with a driver who's been drinking or asking someone aggressive to leave our home are examples of boundaries that we set to protect our physical safety. A restraining order is another example of a boundary that is set, in this case by a judge, to keep someone safe from physical harm. These types of boundaries define how others can treat us and what we'll do to keep ourself safe. If we don't set boundaries, we run the risk of being hurt.

EMOTIONAL SAFETY

Often, the danger we face isn't physical, but emotional. And while emotional pain isn't life-threatening, it's just as real and hurts just as much as physical pain. Our emotional safety is threatened when we're:

- Bullied

- Belittled or called derogatory names

- Frequently criticized

- Lied to

- Blamed for things we didn't do

- Shamed or told we're inadequate

- Yelled at

- Betrayed or cheated on

- With someone unpredictable or prone to angry outbursts

Even an isolated occurrence by a stranger can be painful. But it's even more painful when these types of behaviors are perpetrated regularly by a loved one.

Boundaries are a way to protect ourselves from threats to our emotional safety because they communicate how we expect to be treated and what we'll accept from others. For example, you can set a boundary to maintain emotional safety by hanging up the phone when your sister starts cursing at you or you can ask your father to stop making sarcastic comments about your appearance.

Boundaries Ensure You Focus on What's Most Important

In addition to protecting our physical and emotional safety, boundaries protect us from overworking, overcommitting, over-giving, being taken advantage of, and doing things that don't align with our values and priorities.

If we had unlimited amounts of time, energy, and money, we could say yes to everything. But, since we have limited resources, we need to be thoughtful about how we spend our time, energy, and money. Boundaries serve as limits that ensure we're using our resources on the things that matter most to us. For example, if I say yes to every project I'm asked to do, I'll be overworked, and I won't have enough time and energy for my family. And, since I value quality family time, I need to protect it with a boundary on how many hours I work.

As you can see, saying yes to one thing means you'll have to say no to something else. Conversely, when you say no or set a boundary, it frees up resources for the things you value most.

So far, we've talked about boundaries as dividing lines that differentiate one person from another and clarify what we're each responsible for. Boundaries act as limits that protect us from physical and emotional harm and from spending our time, energy, and money on things we don't value.

How do you define boundaries? Try writing your own definition.

_____

_____

_____

_____

_____

What Happens When We Don't Have Boundaries?

Sometimes the easiest way to understand why boundaries are so important is to think about what happens when we don't have boundaries. Let's look at how Alex and Joaquin are affected by their lack of boundaries.

Alex had just put her two young daughters down for their afternoon nap when the doorbell rang. She immediately felt annoyed because her friends and family all know that her girls nap at this time and she'd even taped a note on the front door that said "Do not disturb." Children napping. Alex's mother stood on her doorstep, her arms overflowing with balloons and bags. "Well, aren't you going to invite me in?" she snapped. "Mom, it's not a good time," Alex said as the baby started crying. Now both girls were up and Alex's plan to catch up on housework and return some emails was quickly evaporating. "I brought you Valentine's Day treats!" her mother said excitedly, emptying packages of candy onto the living room floor. "Thanks, Mom," Alex replied. But she was really thinking, She knows we don't let the girls eat candy. She's always undermining me. Two hours later, Alex's mother was finally gone, leaving a mess of candy wrappers and craft projects, two overtired and cranky grandchildren, and Alex on the verge of tears. Alex wasn't just angry at her mother for disrupting her afternoon or ignoring her wishes; she was also angry at herself for allowing it. She was angry that at thirty-five years old, she still didn't know how to say no to her mother.

Joaquin looked at his schedule and immediately felt overwhelmed. He had counseling sessions with students booked every thirty minutes, a life skills class to teach during lunch, a staff meeting after school, and then his own family to tend to. He momentarily hoped some of his students would be out sick so he could get a break, but immediately felt guilty for being selfish. Joaquin was eager to help—that's why he'd become a school social worker. When there were budget cuts, he agreed to counsel additional students. When the school identified youth vaping as a concern, he volunteered to hold informational seminars for parents in the evenings. He routinely brought home hours of paperwork and was emotionally drained by the struggles the students shared with him. Joaquin became increasingly sleep-deprived. He gave up swimming because he didn't have enough energy. And his relationships suffered because he barely saw his wife and kids. Joaquin wasn't selfish— quite the opposite; he gave and gave at work and had nothing left for himself or his family.

While Alex struggled with boundaries in her personal life, Joaquin didn't set boundaries at work. And both paid a steep price. They were exhausted and felt resentful and taken advantage of. Their relationships suffered. They felt guilty and didn't get their needs met. Joaquin was particularly drained because he didn't have a boundary between his emotions and those of his students; he absorbed their feelings and let them become part of him.

Boundaries Are a Two-Way Street

When it comes to boundary-related problems, we usually think about how we're hurt when we don't set boundaries or when others don't respect our boundaries. But it's important to remember that boundaries are a two-way street. Many of us need to work on respecting other people's boundaries, not just asserting our own boundaries.

When we don't respect other people's boundaries, we can cause them harm. You may not cause physical harm, but you could make someone uncomfortable by intruding on their personal space or privacy. Or you might harm someone by not returning a borrowed item, not following through on a commitment, or "oversharing" too much personal information given how well you know someone.

Now, let's turn our attention to why you want to learn how to set boundaries. Use this checklist to identify how your life is negatively affected by a lack of consistent boundaries.

- ☐ You're afraid to say no and don't want to disappoint people.

- ☐ You don't speak up when you want something or when you're being mistreated.

- ☐ You frequently feel angry, resentful, or overwhelmed.

- ☐ You don't communicate your expectations to others.

- ☐ You feel physically or emotionally unsafe.

- ☐ You don't make time for self-care.

- ☐ You feel guilty when you set limits or do things for yourself.

- ☐ You make commitments that you later regret.

- ☐ You're frequently overscheduled, rushed, or tired.

- ☐ You do things out of obligation rather than because you want to.

- ☐ You don't spend enough quality time with people you care about.

- ☐ You don't have a strong sense of who you are and your values, interests, and goals.

- ☐ You're tuned in to how other people feel, but don't always know how you feel.

- ☐ You accept blame for things you didn't do or couldn't control.

- ☐ You enable others to be irresponsible by doing things for them that they can do for themselves.

- ☐ You feel obligated to answer personal questions.

☐ You loan money or possessions to people who don't return them.

☐ People take advantage of you.

☐ Your children don't respect limits and walk all over you.

☐ Your children act entitled or spoiled.

☐ You feel burnt out at work.

☐ You spend a lot of time, energy, or money trying to fix or solve other people's problems.

☐ You act passive-aggressively instead of directly expressing your feelings and needs.

☐ You think you don't matter or aren't as important as others.

☐ You overshare personal information or get close to people before trust is established.

☐ You blame others for things you're responsible for.

☐ You harm others by not respecting their privacy, possessions, feelings, or bodies.

☐ You struggle with self-discipline (managing your money, time, eating, social media use, etc.).

In what other ways has not having boundaries negatively affected you? (Be as specific as possible.)

_____

_____

_____

_____

_____

_____

It's important to be aware of the ways that not having boundaries has impacted you but looking at a list of problems can certainly be discouraging or overwhelming. So, we're not going to stay focused on the negatives! This book is going to teach you the skills you need to set boundaries and overcome these problems.

The Benefits of Boundaries

Now that you've got a clear picture of the problems that result from poor boundaries, let's look at how boundaries can improve your life, specifically your relationships, health, and self-esteem.

Boundaries Improve Relationships

People often avoid setting boundaries because they're afraid that boundaries will damage their relationships by creating distance or conflict. Indeed, setting boundaries may initially be met with some resistance. However, most people will adjust to your boundaries and your relationships will be strengthened by clearer communication, fewer misunderstandings and conflicts, and greater trust, respect, and connection.

Personal and professional relationships are built on open and honest communication. Boundaries are how we communicate our expectations to others: what we want and need, how we want to be treated, and what actions we'll take if our expectations aren't met. If we don't communicate our expectations and needs, others won't know what we expect from them and what they can expect from us.

Understanding each other's expectations decreases misunderstandings and arguments. For example, if I don't give my teenage son a curfew, but then get angry at him for coming home late, my son will be confused and upset because I didn't make my expectations clear. And he may find it hard to trust me because I didn't set clear boundaries. Setting a boundary, telling him that I expect him home at 11 p.m., is kinder. Even though he may not like the limit, he knows what's expected and that it's his responsibility to be home by 11 p.m. Clear boundaries, such as a curfew for a teenager, foster healthy accountability and minimize blaming, arguing, and misunderstandings.

Setting boundaries also increases the chances that our needs and expectations will be met. Expecting our friends and family to read our minds and know what we want without telling them never works! We need to communicate. And while asking doesn't guarantee that we'll get what we want or need, we're much more likely to get it when we're clear and direct. And when our needs and expectations are met, relationships are easier and more fulfilling.

Boundaries Improve Health

I consider boundaries a form of self-care because they protect us from physical and emotional harm and they safeguard the time, energy, and money that we need to take care of ourselves.

Boundaries are a way to protect yourself from physical harm, such as being hit. Boundaries can also protect you from the mental anguish of enduring another Christmas with your emotionally abusive family or from working late with a coworker who makes unwanted sexual advances. By creating safety, boundaries protect us from stress-related health problems like high blood pressure, heart disease, headaches, and insomnia.

Boundaries are also a self-management tool that help us prioritize healthy habits like getting enough sleep, not drinking too much, and ensuring we have time and energy to exercise. Without boundaries, we're likely to spend our time, energy, and money indiscriminately and there might not be enough left for healthy activities, such as going to therapy or getting a flu shot.

Boundaries Improve Self-Esteem

Being able to assertively communicate your thoughts, feelings, and ideas, and asking for what you want or need is empowering. When you set boundaries, you'll feel more confident. You'll have a stronger sense of who you are and what matters to you. And you'll feel good about standing up for yourself and not letting others take advantage of or mistreat you.

As you learn to set boundaries, you'll also value yourself more. When you do things that support your physical and mental health, your self-esteem grows. You recognize that you have value and that your rights and needs matter just as much as everyone else's.

How do you think boundaries will improve your life? Give some specific examples.

_____

_____

_____

_____

_____

_____

How will boundaries improve your relationships with others?

_____

_____

_____

_____

_____

How will boundaries improve your emotional and physical health?

_____

_____

_____

_____

_____

How will boundaries improve your self-esteem or relationship with yourself?

_____

_____

_____

_____

_____

Even when you see the benefits of boundaries, it's normal to feel apprehensive about making a significant change. So, before we move on, take a few minutes to acknowledge your concerns or worries about setting boundaries.

What concerns do you have about setting boundaries? What has held you back from setting boundaries in the past?

_____

_____

_____

_____

_____

Summary

Often, getting started is the hardest part of learning something new. So, give yourself a gold star! You're off to a great start. In this chapter, you learned about the three primary functions of boundaries: defining who you are and what you're responsible for, protecting yourself from physical and emotional harm, and ensuring that your needs are met by focusing on what's most important to you. And you learned about the benefits of boundaries, including how they can improve relationships, health, and self-esteem. Unfortunately, many of us have gotten mixed messages and misinformation about what boundaries are and what they aren't. So, in chapter 2, we'll dispel some common myths about boundaries.

Chapter 2

What Boundaries Are Not

Chapter 1 gave you an overview of what boundaries are and how they can improve your life. But there's a lot of misinformation circulating about boundaries, so it's also important that we're clear about what boundaries are not.

Common Myths About Boundaries

Let's explore common boundary myths and how to change the negative associations you have about boundaries. This will help you see that your needs are valid and you're worthy of healthy boundaries.

Boundaries Are Not Demands

In the previous chapter, I explained that boundaries are a form of self-care—something you do for yourself. The primary purpose of a boundary is to take care of yourself, not to control others.

When we set boundaries, we often ask someone to change their behavior. But a boundary is simply a request—a way to communicate our needs or expectations—not a demand or an attempt to force someone to do what we want. And although it's normal to want to feel in control, especially when we're in a dangerous, unpredictable, or uncomfortable situation, demands rarely work. If we make demands under the guise of boundaries, they'll be met with resistance, which in turn can make us reluctant to set boundaries because they don't seem to work. Throughout this book, we'll return to the fact that you can only control yourself and you have limited influence over other people, so it's best to put your effort into taking care of yourself rather than trying to change others.

We also want to remember that demands don't build positive connections and feelings. Most people don't like to be told what to do and find it condescending and rude. Asking for what you want or need is more respectful and likely to elicit cooperation and connection.

Boundaries Are Not Ultimatums

Boundaries, also, are not ultimatums or threats. An ultimatum is a final demand and statement about how you'll retaliate against someone if they don't do what you want. An ultimatum is built on a desire to control and punish.

A boundary violation should result in a consequence, not an ultimatum or threat. The distinction between an ultimatum and a consequence can be subtle because it largely reflects our motivations—whether we're trying to punish someone or protect ourselves. The same statement can be an ultimatum or a boundary consequence depending on how and why it's said. See if you can notice the difference in the following example.

Kamal's coworker, Ruby, frequently speaks rudely to him, calling him degrading names and making fun of his accent. Kamal set a boundary to protect himself by saying, "Ruby, it's not okay for you to speak to me this way. When you make fun of me, I feel hurt and embarrassed. I'd like you to stop. And if you continue to make fun of me, I'll make a complaint to human resources."

Did Kamal set a boundary with a consequence or did he issue an ultimatum? It depends. If his goal in reporting Ruby to human resources is to protect himself, it's a consequence. However, if his goal is to get Ruby in trouble or to control her with fear, it's an ultimatum. In contrast, if he had said, "If you continue to make fun of me, I'll leave the room or end the phone call," it would definitely be a consequence and not an ultimatum. Removing himself from the hurtful situation is a way for Kamal to protect himself. Either consequence can be appropriate depending on the particulars of the situation.

Tone of voice is also a good indicator of our motivation. Ultimatums are usually given when we're angry and often aren't well thought out. You may later regret an ultimatum that was given in haste and not follow through with it.

People don't usually respond well to anger and threats, so ultimatums aren't particularly effective in getting people to change. They also tend to damage relationships, shut down communication, and increase anger.

Can you think of a time when you gave or received an ultimatum? Describe what happened.

_____

_____

_____

_____

_____

What could have been said to state a boundary with a consequence instead of an ultimatum?

_____

_____

_____

_____

_____

How can you avoid giving ultimatums?

_____

_____

_____

_____

_____

How does it feel to accept that you can't make people do what you want—even when you set boundaries?

_____

_____

_____

_____

_____

Boundaries Are Not Mean

One of the big reasons we avoid setting boundaries is that we mistakenly think they're mean and will lead to conflict and disconnection. But boundaries are inherently respectful because they communicate our expectations and help others understand how to interact with us—what's okay and what's not okay. This decreases misunderstandings and sets the stage for direct and clear communication. In her book *Rising Strong*, Brené Brown explains that she was surprised to discover that people with well-defined boundaries are the most compassionate:

"Compassionate people ask for what they need. They say no when they need to, and when they say yes, they mean it. They're compassionate because their boundaries keep them out of resentment" (Brown 2015, 115).

Boundaries actually make relationships easier. If this seems confusing, think about what it's like when other people set boundaries with you. Don't you appreciate it when your boss sets clear boundaries and tells you specifically what she expects? The same holds in other relationships—kids do best when parents set clear boundaries; intimate relationships and friendships are easier when both parties are direct about their needs and expectations. When we don't set boundaries, we often become resentful and angry, which isn't good for us or our relationships. Boundaries communicate our needs and expectations—and it's kind, not mean, to tell others how we want to be treated, what we need, and what we expect.

Have you experienced setting or receiving boundaries as mean? If so, what do you think made the experience feel unkind?

_____

_____

_____

_____

_____

Can you imagine setting or receiving boundaries as an act of kindness? What would that sound like or what would the situation be?

_____

_____

_____

_____

_____

What would make the difference between a boundary feeling mean and feeling kind?

_____

_____

_____

_____

_____

Boundaries Are Not Selfish

Just because boundaries protect your well-being doesn't mean they're selfish. Everyone has a basic right to feel safe and protect themselves and their resources (property, time, energy, money). It's not selfish to look out for yourself—it's self-preservation.

Being selfish means that you *only* think about yourself. But healthy boundaries consider your needs *and* other people's needs. You're thoughtfully considering what someone else needs as well as your own needs and resources before deciding what you can do or give.

Sometimes, being selfless, or having no concern for your well-being, is seen as an ideal that people should strive for. But selflessness is also problematic because when you neglect yourself, you inevitably get exhausted, sick, and resentful. And, ironically, when you take better care of yourself, you have more to give to others. Self-care has a trickle-down effect because when more of your needs are met, you're happier and healthier, which allows you to be a more patient parent or a more attentive spouse. When you don't take care of yourself, your fatigue, irritability, and physical aches and pains don't just negatively affect you; they negatively affect those around you.

Setting boundaries often creates feelings of guilt—the belief that you've done something wrong. Perhaps you've even been told by your spouse or parents that saying no to their needs or wants is selfish. But setting a boundary and not being able to meet someone else's needs isn't necessarily selfish, as you'll see in Colin's story.

> Colin goes to the gym at 6 a.m. every day. He started this routine at his doctor's recommendation after suffering several panic attacks that landed him in the emergency room. Exercise helps Colin manage his anxiety, and he prioritizes his daily workout because it's the only thing that has reduced his panic attacks. So, when Colin's father asked him to drive him to the airport at 6:15 a.m., Colin set a boundary by saying that he wasn't available. Colin's father pushed back against the boundary in an irritated tone by saying, "I ask you for one thing and you can't be bothered. Your precious workout is more important than your father! You're so selfish, Colin."

Shaming someone, such as calling them selfish, is often an attempt to control them. In this case, Colin's dad tried to convince him that going to the gym was selfish, so he'd feel guilty and take him to the airport. But Colin considered his father's need and his own and concluded that his exercise was more important. Perhaps it's not Colin but his dad who is being selfish by not considering Colin's needs. Or we might choose to avoid the word "selfish" altogether because it tends to be shaming and judgmental. Instead, we could think of Colin and his dad as two people who have competing needs. They are both valid and one person's needs aren't more important than the other's.

Think of a time when the fear of being selfish kept you from setting boundaries. Did you consider other people's needs or wants even if you weren't able to meet them? Describe what happened.

_____

_____

_____

_____

In the situation you described, what would be the middle ground between selfish and selfless? How would it feel?

_____

_____

_____

_____

If it's hard to stop thinking of boundaries as selfish, you can use affirmations to reinforce a new way of thinking. An affirmation is a statement that affirms your right and responsibility to take care of yourself and to value your needs and wants. Here are a few examples of affirmations that Colin might use:

"It's healthy, not selfish, for me to maintain my exercise routine."

"It's okay to prioritize my own needs."

"I'm not responsible for my father's feelings."

Try writing your own affirmations for the situation you identified earlier.

_____

_____

_____

_____

How will setting boundaries and prioritizing your self-care have a positive impact on your loved ones?

_____

_____

_____

_____

Boundaries Are Not Fixed

Boundaries need to be flexible, not fixed. We can't set the same boundaries in every situation or with every person. Instead, the most effective boundaries flex to accommodate different situations, different relationships, and our changing needs, and will get fine-tuned as we learn what works and what doesn't.

If we create boundaries that are too rigid, we run the risk of isolating ourselves. Imagine a solid twelve-foot-high brick wall encircling you. It provides excellent protection, but there's no way for others to come in or for you to leave. Often, this happens when we've been hurt (physically or emotionally)—we wall ourselves off in an effort to feel safe. We create rigid boundaries that don't let anyone else into our lives, and we don't share anything vulnerable or communicate our needs. This creates physical and emotional isolation. Instead, we want to be able to strengthen or soften our boundaries as needed so we can discern who's trustworthy and let them into our lives. Flexible boundaries are like a gate that we open and close; we can adjust who and how much we let in.

As you can see in the following table, weak boundaries leave us vulnerable to being hurt and rigid boundaries lead to isolation or disconnection from others. Our goal is flexible boundaries that promote respectful, mutually satisfying relationships.

	Weak or No Boundaries	Flexible or Healthy Boundaries	Rigid or Overly Tight Boundaries
How you feel	Vulnerable	Safe and connected	Isolated
How others treat you	Others are likely to hurt you.	Others treat you with respect and connect in ways that feel good.	Others can't approach or connect with you.
How you treat others	You're likely to hurt others.	You treat others with respect and connect in ways that feel good to them.	You don't approach or try to connect with others.

And while we want our boundaries to be flexible, we still need them to be clear and firm. At any given moment, you can clearly set limits and ask for what you want or need. And you also have the right to change your mind and to set different limits with different people or with the same person in different situations. For example, Mark is comfortable with more physical touch from his spouse at home versus in public. If his boundaries weren't flexible, he'd be limited to either too much physical touch in public (making him feel uncomfortable) or too little physical touch in private (making him feel neglected or unfulfilled).

Do you tend to have boundaries that are too rigid or too weak? Describe your boundaries.

_____

_____

_____

_____

_____

What kinds of problems have boundaries that are too rigid or too weak caused?

_____

_____

_____

_____

_____

Identify two or three situations where it would be helpful for you to have flexible boundaries.

_____

_____

_____

_____

_____

Reframing Your Ideas About Boundaries

The following table summarizes what boundaries are and are not. It can help you challenge any negative associations you may have about boundaries and remind you that boundaries are both good and necessary. If you think of additional positive aspects of boundaries, add them in the blank spaces provided.

Boundaries Are	Boundaries Are Not
Well thought out, clear, and direct	Impulsive or reactive
Statements or actions that express what you need or want	Attempts to control or punish others
Limits that protect your health, safety, and resources	Ultimatums or threats
Kind	Nagging, criticizing, or being disrespectful
Self-care	Selfish
Choices that help you feel safe	Attempts to limit other people's choices or freedom

Summary

In this chapter, we began to challenge some of the myths about boundaries—that boundaries are demanding, mean, selfish, and fixed. And as you work through this book, you'll repeatedly see that learning to set boundaries isn't about convincing or forcing others to do what you want; boundaries are about expressing yourself clearly, asking for what you need, and honoring your needs by making choices that support your well-being. Next, we'll work through some of the obstacles that make setting boundaries so hard.

Chapter 3

Why It's Hard to Set Boundaries

We all know that setting boundaries is hard, but have you ever wondered why? Understanding what makes it hard for you to set healthy boundaries will help you change the thoughts and behaviors that are getting in your way. In this chapter, you'll learn about the four most common barriers to setting boundaries and how to overcome these challenges and feel better about yourself, your needs, and your right to set boundaries.

No One Taught You How to Set Boundaries

One reason that we struggle to set boundaries is that we're not familiar with them. We didn't see others setting boundaries. We weren't told that we have the right to set boundaries. And we weren't taught how to set boundaries or encouraged to do so.

For the most part, we learn about boundaries by watching others—our parents, friends, coworkers, and even fictional characters in books and movies. Our parents or caretakers usually have the greatest influence on us because we spend considerable time with them, especially when we're young and most impressionable. We watch how they resolve conflicts, how they ask for what they need, how they allow others to treat them, and how they treat themselves. These become our models for understanding and setting boundaries.

Setting boundaries is a skill, just like cooking or driving a car, so if no one taught you how to set them and gave you opportunities to practice, it makes sense that you're still learning and perhaps feeling rather unskilled.

You may want to pause here and take some time to reflect on who influenced your boundaries.

Who modeled healthy boundaries for you? (If you can't think of anyone that you knew in person, there might be a character from a book or show.) Describe what these boundaries were like.

_____

_____

_____

_____

_____

Who modeled unhealthy boundaries for you? Describe what these boundaries were like.

_____

_____

_____

_____

_____

Very unhealthy boundaries are one sign that a family is dysfunctional. As you continue reading, you'll learn more about the connection between unhealthy boundaries and other family problems.

Boundaries in Dysfunctional Families

"Dysfunctional family" is a broad term that refers to families with chronic problems (such as addiction, anger and controlling behaviors, lack of empathy, or poor boundaries) that negatively affect family members. Dysfunction exists on a continuum—no family functions perfectly, of course, and unfortunately, many people have families that seriously damage their physical and mental health.

Communication is one area where dysfunctional families struggle. They rarely use the assertive communication skills needed for healthy boundaries. Instead, boundaries are too rigid, too weak, or nonexistent, and communication is aggressive (is harsh and disrespectful), passive (avoids talking about feelings, problems, or difficult subjects), or passive-aggressive (displays anger without directly specifying the issue). Many people grow up not realizing that assertive communication—directly and respectfully expressing an opinion or asking for what they want—is even possible. Assertive communication is essential to setting boundaries; in chapter 5, you'll learn how to assertively communicate your boundaries. But first, let's explore how rigid or weak boundaries in childhood set us up for problems setting boundaries in adulthood.

FAMILIES WITH RIGID BOUNDARIES

Parents with rigid boundaries have inflexible rules and harsh consequences. The rules or limits are a one-size-fits-all approach and are not always age-appropriate (younger children are expected to do things that they aren't developmentally capable of and older children aren't given more privacy or independence as they mature). Parents with rigid boundaries don't make exceptions to their rules, like extending curfew for a teenager on prom night or understanding that a child's grades slipped because we experienced a pandemic. When boundaries are rigid, there's little opportunity for children to explore their identities and individuality because the emphasis is on doing what you're told and meeting external expectations. The consequences of noncompliance tend to be harsh and inflexible.

If you grew up in a family with rigid boundaries, you may have felt controlled, micromanaged, and misunderstood. You probably weren't encouraged to set limits with others or figure out what you needed. And because your parents always told you what to do, you may find it difficult to set limits for yourself as an adult, such as going to bed on time or limiting your use of social media.

It may have been difficult to connect with your parents and feel close to them due to their rigid boundaries. They probably weren't very good at noticing and tending to your feelings. Rigid parenting boundaries can lack empathy because they don't consider the individual child's needs and feelings.

Rigid boundaries also make it difficult for "outsiders" to enter the family system. The outsider could be a new boyfriend, teacher, neighbor, or rabbi. They aren't welcomed warmly but treated with skepticism and mistrust. Rigid boundaries provide protection (although the protection isn't always needed) and make it hard to form relationships outside the family. This can lead to family secrets, shame, and the belief that family ties matter above all other relationships and should never be broken.

When the adults in your life treat everyone as a threat, you don't learn how to determine for yourself who is trustworthy and safe. You see the world as black or white—people as good or evil, trustworthy or predator, friend or enemy. You struggle to be vulnerable in relationships and probably recreate rigid boundaries out of fear and familiarity.

FAMILIES WITH WEAK BOUNDARIES

Families with weak or no boundaries are unsafe. Children aren't given consistent age-appropriate rules or limits to keep them safe, so a toddler might play in the street unsupervised or eat unlimited cookies. A lack of respect for physical, emotional, and sexual boundaries can lead to abuse by family members or by unsafe people who are allowed into the home. If you grew up in a family with weak boundaries, you probably learned that you can't trust your parents to keep you safe. You experience the world as unpredictable and scary. As an adult, you may struggle to trust that you can keep yourself safe.

Weak boundaries also create confusion about who is responsible for what. This can be as simple as confusion about who's responsible for taking out the trash because the expectation was never made clear, or it can be as extreme as a young child taking on adult responsibilities such as childcare or cooking because her parents are unwilling or unable. Families with weak boundaries are also characterized by high levels of blame because expectations aren't clear. Inevitably, children get blamed for things that they didn't do or couldn't control. For example, your mother might blame you for her migraines even though you can't control whether she gets a headache.

Weak boundaries can also lead to enmeshment, or a lack of emotional separation between people. This can include being expected to think, feel, and be like your parents, not being able to explore your individuality, or having your parents inappropriately share too much personal information with you, such as details about their sex life or financial problems.

Families with weak boundaries teach us that we don't have personal rights and shouldn't set boundaries. Boundaries are seen as selfish and mean. You're expected to sacrifice your needs and interests to make others happy, so you come to believe that your needs and feelings aren't important. You may also become overly responsible, feeling responsible for other people's feelings and choices and going to lengths to help or rescue them.

It's also possible that your family had a combination of rigid and weak boundaries. Some families shift back and forth as stressors, mental health conditions, and addictions ebb and flow. Others maintain elements of both extremes.

Did your childhood family have rigid or weak boundaries or a mix of both? Were boundaries and rules consistent or inconsistent, flexible or inflexible, clear or confusing? What was that like for you as a child?

_____

_____

_____

_____

_____

How have the boundary problems in your childhood family made it difficult for you to set boundaries now? Did they impact your communication style, self-esteem, sense of safety, or ability to trust?

_____

_____

_____

_____

_____

_____

Setting Boundaries Is Scary

When I ask people why setting boundaries is hard, the most common answer is fear. Asserting your individuality, asking for what you need, and setting limits can be scary because you've tried and gotten poor results or because setting boundaries is a new skill and you're not sure how to do it or what the outcome will be. Using the checklist below, identify the fears you have about setting boundaries.

I have a fear of:

☐ Hurting someone's feelings

☐ Conflict or anger

☐ Physical abuse

☐ Being ignored

☐ Being misunderstood

☐ Being criticized, ridiculed, or not being taken seriously

☐ Disappointing or displeasing someone

☐ Losing a relationship (rejection or abandonment)

☐ Giving in or not being able to maintain my boundaries

☐ Being unworthy of respect

☐ Realizing my loved one doesn't care about me

Are you surprised by how many fears you have about setting boundaries? This is common and understandable! Often, we feel stuck but don't know exactly what's holding us back. Simply acknowledging your fears is a helpful step and prepares you for our next task—determining whether your fears are accurate.

Fears Are Not Always Accurate

Our fears feel real, but they aren't always accurate. Fears are often based on misperceptions, or what psychologists call cognitive distortions. Humans have a negativity bias, or a tendency to remember negative experiences more than positive ones and a tendency to overestimate the likelihood of negative outcomes. This primes your brain to be fearful, which, in the face of real danger, is useful, but can be a barrier to setting boundaries.

Yes, some fears are based on past experiences. But even these fears are often overgeneralized. For example, if your father yelled at you whenever you attempted to set a boundary with him, you may have become timid about setting boundaries with everyone. The logical part of your mind probably realizes that not everyone will get angry when you set a boundary, but fear can easily override logic and convince you to play it safe or maintain the status quo. Of course, sometimes setting boundaries can put you in danger. Safety is always paramount. Please see chapter 11 for information about staying safe when setting boundaries with difficult people.

We need to be able to look at our fears rationally and determine whether they're accurate and helpful. One way to do this is to look for cognitive distortions in our thinking. Everyone has distorted thoughts; they're common and nothing to be ashamed of. Following are some of the most prevalent types of cognitive distortions, based on the work of Albert Ellis, Aaron Beck, and David Burns. A copy of this list is also available at http://www.newharbinger.com/47582.

- **Discounting the positives:** You notice and focus only on the negatives and minimize or ignore anything good that you do or that happens to you.

  Example: My friend compliments me on being more assertive, but I don't see any progress; I can't stop thinking about how I let Isaiah interrupt me.

- **Overgeneralizing:** You apply one experience to all situations.

  Example: Nothing ever works out for me.

- **All-or-nothing thinking:** You see things as absolutes, there are no in-betweens.

  Example: I can't set boundaries.

- **Mind reading:** You assume others are thinking the same thing you are.

  Example: I'm sure she hates me.

- **Double standard:** You hold yourself to a higher standard than everyone else.

  Example: It's okay if you're not available to help me, but I should always be available when you need something.

- **Catastrophizing:** You expect the worst.

  Example: If I tell Javi he can't smoke in my house, he'll break up with me.

- **Labeling:** You label yourself negatively.

  Example: I'm selfish.

- **Magical thinking:** You think everything will be better when _____ (you're thinner, richer, get a new job, etc.).

  Example: Everything will be better once my kids finally move out.

- **Should-statements:** You judge and criticize yourself for what you should be doing.

  Example: I shouldn't let anyone down (adapted from Martin 2019, 54–55).

Tip	Cognitive distortions often include these words:				
	Everyone	No one	Nobody	All	Every
	Always	Never	Should	Must	Ought

Challenging Your Fear

If fear has been impeding your ability to set boundaries, use the exercise that follows to challenge your fear-based beliefs and determine whether they're accurate.

Identify your fear. If I set boundaries, _____.

Example: If I set boundaries, everyone will hate me.

Identify the underlying belief. I believe _____

_____.

Example: I believe I'm difficult and people don't like me.

Identify the cognitive distortion(s). _____

Example: All-or-nothing thinking, mind reading, catastrophizing.

Once we recognize that our thoughts are distorted, we can work on changing them. To figure out whether your thoughts are accurate or distorted, think of yourself as a scientist or detective looking for evidence to support your beliefs. The following questions can help you do this. A copy of these questions is also available at http://www.newharbinger.com/47582.

- What evidence do I have to support this thought or belief?
- Is this thought or belief based on facts or opinions?
- Do I have a trusted friend who I can check out these thoughts with?
- Is this thought helpful?

- Are there other ways that I can think about this situation or myself?

- Am I blaming myself unnecessarily?

- What or who else contributed to this situation?

- Is it really in my control?

- Am I overgeneralizing?

- Am I making assumptions or jumping to conclusions?

- What would I say to a friend in this situation?

- Can I look for "shades of gray"?

- Am I assuming the worst?

- Am I holding myself to an unreasonable or double standard?

- Are there exceptions to these absolutes (always, never)?

- Am I making this personal when it isn't?

- Who gets to decide what I have to or should do?

- Does this align with my values?

- Is this a realistic expectation? (Adapted from Martin 2019, 58–59.)

Record evidence for or against the underlying belief that you identified in the previous exercise.

_____

_____

_____

Example: Paul got angry when I told him I wasn't going to his parents' with him. I stand up for myself at work and they seem to respect me. I get along with my roommate, so everyone doesn't find me difficult.

Rewrite your fear as a more accurate and supportive statement.

_____

_____

_____

Example: Some people may get angry when I set boundaries with them. But some people do respect my boundaries. Setting boundaries doesn't make me difficult.

I encourage you to download the worksheet Challenging Your Fears at http://www.newharbinger .com/47582 and repeat this exercise for each of your fears about setting boundaries.

Fear isn't the only obstacle to setting boundaries that's based on distorted thoughts. Next, we're going to talk about guilt, another feeling that's often the result of unrealistic expectations and under-valuing ourselves.

Setting Boundaries Makes You Feel Guilty

Guilt is the feeling you have when you think you've done something wrong. So, when you feel guilty about setting boundaries, it's because you don't think you have the right to protect yourself, say no, have your own ideas, or ask for something.

Here are some of the underlying beliefs that can lead to feeling guilty about setting boundaries. Which ones resonate with you?

- ☐ I shouldn't need or want anything.

- ☐ If I do need or want something, I shouldn't ask for it.

- ☐ It's my responsibility to take care of others.

- ☐ Being selfless is a virtue.

- ☐ I should always put others before myself.

- ☐ I should keep my opinions to myself. No one wants to hear them.

- ☐ What I want doesn't matter.

- ☐ It's mean, rude, or wrong to say no.

- ☐ It's selfish to consider my own needs.

These beliefs are all based on an inequitable relationship where another person's rights and needs are assumed to be more important than yours. Boundaries are built on the idea that we all have the same rights and that you matter as much as everyone else. Guilt, on the other hand, comes from the belief that boundaries are wrong or that you don't deserve to set boundaries.

If you struggle to set boundaries, it may be because you directly or indirectly got the message that you aren't important and don't deserve to be treated well, your needs or feelings don't matter or should come second, you shouldn't ask for anything (and if you do, you won't get it or will be ignored or shamed for asking), and some people matter more than others.

Have you ever thought that you don't have the right to set boundaries? That you don't deserve to be treated with respect? Or that you're not worth the effort? If so, where do you think these beliefs came from?

_____

_____

_____

_____

_____

_____

Personal Rights in Your Daily Life

I want you to consider that we all have the same personal rights and that you matter as much as everyone else. This may be hard to believe; it may be very different than what you learned from your parents, religious teachings, or culture. Those can be strong messages to challenge. But doing so is the key to being able to treat yourself with love and respect—and to ask the same from others. You won't be able to set boundaries if you continue to feel unworthy or undeserving.

When you make choices out of guilt, you're letting someone else decide what's right or wrong for you; you're letting their ideas dictate how you should live your life. But accepting that you have the same personal rights as everyone else means you have the right to make your own choices as a mature adult who knows what's best for yourself.

Following are some examples of personal rights. I encourage you to add to the list, being as specific as possible to make it useful to you. I also recommend downloading an additional copy of Identifying and Accepting Your Personal Rights from http://www.newharbinger.com/47582 and reviewing it regularly.

- I have the right to be treated with respect and kindness.

- I have the right to say no.

- I have the right to change my mind.

- I have the right to be physically and emotionally safe.

- I have the right to have my own thoughts, feelings, values, and beliefs.

- I have the right to happiness and pleasure.

- I have the right to rest.

- I have the right to privacy.

- I have the right to share or not share my possessions.

- I have the right to decide what's best for me.

- I have the right to distance myself from or end relationships with negative or hurtful people.

- I have the right to pursue my goals.

- I have the right to set boundaries.

- I have the right to _____.

- I have the right to _____.

- I have the right to _____.

Some people object to the idea of personal rights because they're afraid they will become selfish or controlling. But the premise is that your rights are *as important* as everyone else's, not that your rights are *more important*. As a relational creature, you need to consider other people's needs and preferences, but if they consistently supersede yours, you're accepting a "less than" position in the relationship and reinforcing the belief that you matter less than others. Boundaries and personal rights help bring relationships back into balance.

Are any of these personal rights difficult for you to accept? Why do you think that is?

_____

_____

_____

_____

_____

_____

If a friend told you that she didn't think she had the right to _____ (fill in the blank with any of the personal rights that you struggle with), what would you say to her?

_____

_____

_____

_____

_____

_____

Now, try telling yourself the same thing to reinforce that these personal rights apply to you, too. Saying kind, encouraging things to yourself is an effective way to reduce self-critical or self-defeating thoughts (such as *I don't deserve to be happy* or *My needs don't matter*) (Neff 2011). Rewrite what you'd say to a friend so you can practice saying it to yourself.

_____

_____

_____

_____

_____

_____

It takes regular practice to change your thoughts, so you'll get the best results if you repeat or write down this statement at least once a day for the next several weeks.

Another way to recognize your inherent worth is to treat yourself with respect and kindness. You can do this through actions and words. When you prioritize your needs (perhaps scheduling time to see friends or go to the dentist), you show yourself (and others) that you matter. To put this into practice, deliberately do three acts of self-care every day. They don't need to be glamorous or time-consuming, but they do need to be meaningful and intentional.

What three self-care activities will you do today?

1. _____

2. _____

3. _____

For maximum benefit, record your three self-care activities daily and as you do them, say to yourself, *I'm doing this because I matter*. This will bring more conscious awareness to your thoughts and actions and reinforce their purpose.

To continue building your self-worth and confidence in your personal rights, fill in the following table with specific examples of what your personal rights look like in your life.

Personal Right	What does this personal right look like in your daily life?
Example: I have a right to privacy.	No one should read my email without permission. I'll close my bedroom door when I want privacy.

You Don't Know Who You Are or What You Need

If you don't have a clear sense of who you are and what you need, it can be difficult to set boundaries. Your boundaries are unique to you, based on the personal rights discussed earlier and your needs and preferences. For example, I might need more personal space than you do. Boundaries aren't as simple as saying we all need to sit three feet apart from each other. With some people and in some situations, you may want to sit closer than three feet and in other situations, you may want more distance. But if you don't know what you need or want, you can't ask for it or even meet the need for yourself. Likewise, if you don't know what matters to you or what your goals are, you can't set boundaries to protect them.

Not knowing who you are or what you need can be both the result and the cause of boundary difficulties. Families with rigid or weak boundaries don't encourage individuation, the age-appropriate process of children separating emotionally and physically from their parents as they mature. Instead, your self-esteem becomes contingent on pleasing others. When you don't have a strong sense of self-worth, you rely on other people's validation and approval to make you feel good about yourself.

Getting to Know Yourself

If you grew up in a family that struggled with boundaries, you may not have been allowed to explore what you like, express differing opinions or beliefs, or try new things. You also may not have felt understood or valued as an individual. And if your parents didn't adequately notice and meet your needs, you may have subconsciously learned that your needs don't matter. You may not have learned how to pay attention to your feelings and the body sensations that tell you what you need.

Building self-esteem and self-understanding is an ongoing process. It's not something you can accomplish in a week or a month. Answering the following questions is a way to start the process.

What are you good at?

_____

_____

What are your short-term goals? Long-term goals?

_____

_____

Who matters most to you?

_____

_____

Who can you go to for support or help?

_____

_____

What do you like to do for fun?

_____

_____

What do you value? What do you believe in?

_____

_____

Where or when do you feel safest?

_____

_____

What or who gives you comfort?

_____

_____

What are you passionate about?

_____

_____

What are you grateful for?

_____

_____

How do you know that you're feeling stressed or upset?

_____

_____

How do you learn best (doing, watching, listening, reading)?

_____

_____

What makes you feel respected?

_____

_____

What makes you feel loved?

_____

_____

What makes you feel safe?

_____

_____

Another strategy for getting to know yourself is to keep a record of your likes and dislikes. This is a simple way to learn more about your preferences, personality, and needs, which will later help you identify boundaries that will increase your life satisfaction.

Date	Likes	Dislikes
Example: March 1	Being the first one up in the morning Bringing lunch from home Having coffee with Surya	Long meetings Mel micromanaging me Coming home to a messy house

Getting to know and feel good about yourself is a big undertaking—and you're off to a great start! I encourage you to continue working on this chart and the previous questions (you can download extra copies of the Getting to Know Yourself questions at http://www.newharbinger.com/47582). By continuing to get to know yourself and recognizing your personal rights, you'll gradually develop a greater sense of self-worth, which will help you feel more confident and less guilty about setting boundaries.

Quick Tips for Building Self-Esteem

- Speak to yourself with kindness, as you'd speak to a dear friend.

- Identify your strengths and ways to use them.

- Forgive yourself for making mistakes.

- Give yourself plenty of healthy treats (get creative and think beyond food).

- Read daily affirmations or inspirational quotes.

- Try not to compare yourself to others.

- Set achievable goals.

- Spend time doing things you enjoy.

- Focus on what you can control or change.

- Write down your successes.

- Write down the progress (no matter how small) you've made toward a goal.

- Do something nice for a friend or an animal.

- Accept compliments.

- Challenge self-critical thoughts. Ask yourself: Is it helpful, kind, and accurate?

- Strive to learn something new every day.

- Do something that you're good at.

Identifying Your Needs

To remain physically and emotionally healthy, we all need various things, such as food, sleep, safety, and respect. In chapter 1, we talked about how boundaries help us meet our need for safety by limiting our exposure to harmful people and situations. Boundaries can help us meet many of our other needs as well.

Unfortunately, many of us aren't aware of our needs or we try to minimize them or pretend we don't have any needs. To set useful and effective boundaries, we must become more aware and accepting of our needs.

When thinking about your needs, it's important to remember these two facts:

1. Everyone has needs—and having needs doesn't make you "needy."

2. Meeting your needs is necessary for your health and well-being; it's not selfish.

Following is a list of some universal human needs. As you read through them, circle the needs that you're experiencing and add additional needs that you can think of. Universal human needs include:

- Physical safety
- Emotional safety
- Respect
- Appreciation
- Love
- Acceptance
- Understanding
- Trust
- Honesty
- Kindness
- Help or support
- Physical touch
- Connection

- Privacy or time alone
- Fun
- Quiet
- Excitement or novelty
- Creative outlets
- To be challenged
- Food and water
- Rest and sleep
- Independence or autonomy
- Spiritual connection
- _____
- _____
- _____

Summary

In this chapter, we explored four common barriers to setting boundaries: 1) not having someone teach or model healthy boundaries for you, 2) fear, 3) guilt, and 4) not knowing yourself or what you need. You learned how the boundaries (or a lack of boundaries) in your childhood family influenced your current boundaries, how to challenge your fears about setting boundaries, that you have personal rights, and more about who you are. You've now completed part one! The work you've done so far will give you a solid foundation for learning how to set effective boundaries.

Part Two

SETTING EFFECTIVE BOUNDARIES

Chapter 4

How to Set Boundaries

Now that you have a good understanding of what boundaries are, how they can improve your life, and how to overcome many of the obstacles to setting healthy boundaries, you're ready to practice creating and setting boundaries.

There are a lot of exercises in this chapter—more than you can probably do in one sitting. I recommend scheduling several blocks of uninterrupted time over the next week or two to focus on this chapter. Working at a slower pace takes some of the pressure off and allows the material to sink in and get integrated. After each section, you may want to pause and check in with yourself. If you feel stressed, overwhelmed, or tired, take a break and recenter yourself (perhaps listen to your favorite music, take a nap, exercise, or give yourself a small treat).

Four Steps to Setting Better Boundaries

In this chapter, you'll learn a four-step formula for setting boundaries inspired by the work of Vicki Tidwell Palmer (2016). This formula will help you figure out what boundaries you need and how to put them into action.

Step 1: Clarify What You Need and Want

Your boundaries must meet your unique needs, so I can't simply give you a list of generic boundaries and expect they will meet your requirements. Therefore, the first step in setting boundaries is to clarify what you need and want. Ask yourself the following four questions:

1. What boundary-related problems am I experiencing?

2. What are my unmet needs?

3. How do I feel?

4. What outcome do I want? What do I want to accomplish with my boundaries?

Identifying your boundary-related problems, unmet needs, and feelings will help you clarify what you hope to accomplish by setting boundaries.

WHAT BOUNDARY-RELATED PROBLEMS ARE YOU EXPERIENCING?

Understanding the problems that you're experiencing due to weak, rigid, or inconsistent boundaries will give you important information about what you need and want—and ultimately help you identify the boundaries that you need to set. When describing your boundary problems, try to be specific and stay focused on one problem or situation at a time.

Describe one of your boundary-related problems.

Example: My friend Rachel is consistently twenty to thirty minutes late when we get together.

_____

_____

_____

Often, boundary-related problems are obvious. They tend to be recurring and cause us a great deal of distress. However, sometimes it's hard to pinpoint what the problem is. You might have a gut feeling or general sense that something's off, but you can't identify what it is. This is okay, and later in this chapter, I'll show you how to use these feelings to identify boundary-related problems.

WHAT ARE YOUR UNMET NEEDS?

When you experience boundary-related problems, like the one you just identified, there's an underlying unmet need, something that you need but aren't getting, which is causing you distress or discomfort. Identifying these unmet needs will give you valuable information about what boundaries to set.

Using the same boundary-related problem and the list of universal needs from chapter 3 (also available in the Appendix), identify your unmet needs.

Problem: Rachel is consistently late.

Unmet need(s): Respect.

Problem: _____

Unmet need(s): _____

HOW DO YOU FEEL?

Your feelings can also alert you to boundary problems and unmet needs. Feelings are like signposts; if we pay attention to them, they'll tell us what we need. Take a moment to think about how you feel when your boundaries are violated—perhaps angry, hurt, afraid, or uncomfortable. Paying attention to such feelings is another way to recognize boundary-related problems and unmet needs.

We can work backward when we feel angry, hurt, afraid, or uncomfortable and determine whether a boundary violation may have led to these feelings. Here's an example: I was sitting in my office and noticed that I felt annoyed. I reflected on what happened that may have contributed to this feeling and remembered that my coworker had barged in without knocking, interrupting me. She violated my need for respect, privacy, and quiet. In this situation, noticing my feelings helped me recognize that my coworker had crossed a boundary and that setting a boundary would help me meet my need for respect, privacy, and quiet.

As in this example, you'll have the most success when you notice your feelings right away. The more time that elapses between the boundary problem and noticing your feelings, the harder it becomes to connect the two.

There are, of course, many possible reasons for our feelings, and boundary violations aren't always what's behind them. But even if you discover that your feelings aren't pointing you toward a boundary issue, it's helpful to pay more attention to your feelings and be aware of what they're telling you.

In particular, pay attention to the following feelings, as they're common emotional responses to boundary violations:

Angry	Afraid	Hurt	Uncomfortable
Resentful	Scared	Sad	Uneasy
Frustrated	Terrified	Depressed	Awkward
Annoyed	Worried	Hopeless	Tense
Irritated	Distressed	Miserable	On edge
Pissed		Upset	Embarrassed
Mad		Unimportant	Ashamed
Furious			
Livid			
Outraged			
Bothered			

Identify how you felt when you experienced the boundary-related problem that you've identified.

Problem: *Rachel is consistently late.*

Feeling(s): *Annoyed, disrespected, unimportant.*

Problem: _____

Feeling(s): _____

WHAT OUTCOME DO YOU WANT?

Once you've identified the problem, your unmet needs, and your feelings, you can put them together to create a clear statement about the outcome you want when you set this boundary. I've found that using the specific formula below is the most effective way to clarify what I truly need and want.

I need _____ (need) and want to feel _____ (feeling) when _____ (situation).

You'll notice that you aren't focusing on how to achieve this yet, only on what you need and how you want to feel.

Now, incorporate the problems, needs, and feelings you've identified into this formula to create your desired outcome statement. *Tip:* The way you want to feel is usually the opposite of how you feel when this problem occurs. You can download lists of positive and unpleasant feelings at http://www.newharbinger.com/47582.

Example: I need respect and want to feel at ease, respected, and valued when I get together with Rachel.

I need _____ (need) and want to feel _____ (feeling)

when _____ (situation).

Now that you know *what* you want to achieve, you can figure out *how* to create your desired outcome.

Step 2: Identify Your Boundaries

Step 2 is identifying the specific boundaries that will help you achieve your desired outcome. In most cases, there are multiple ways to meet your needs and create positive feelings. First you'll identify all your options and then you'll choose the right one for you by examining what is within your control.

WHAT ARE YOUR OPTIONS?

It's important to identify as many options as possible. Don't limit yourself to what you think is possible or what seems like a good solution. Brainstorm without judging or editing. Try to identify five to ten options for each boundary you need to set.

Here's a list of possible options for handling Rachel's chronic tardiness:

- Stop hanging out with Rachel.

- Get together less frequently.

- Only get together with Rachel when I have plenty of free time.

- Don't go to anything with a firm start time (like the movies) with Rachel.

- Tell Rachel that we're meeting thirty minutes before the actual start time.

- Arrive late myself.

- Leave if she's more than fifteen minutes late.

- Start without her and stick to a firm end time.

- Ask her to be on time.

- Do nothing and accept that Rachel will be late.

List all the ways that you can meet the unmet needs that you identified in step 1.

_____

_____

_____

_____

_____

_____

_____

_____

WHAT CAN YOU CONTROL?

When deciding how to best meet our needs, we need to determine whether we can meet these needs ourselves or whether we have to ask someone else to help us. We can usually meet some of our needs ourselves, but other needs are relational by nature and we may have to ask someone to change their behavior or help us. So, when you're deciding what boundaries to set, consider what's in your control and what's not.

You can control your own words, actions, feelings, and thoughts. You can't control what other people say, do, feel, or think. This seems straightforward, but most of us mistakenly think we have more control or influence over others than we actually do. As a result, we waste a lot of time trying to get people to say, do, feel, and think the way we want them to. Once we accept that we can't make others do what we want—including respecting our boundaries—we can focus on what we can do to meet our needs or how we can communicate them in ways that build cooperative relationships.

When you look at the options for dealing with Rachel's tardiness and the brainstorming list that you made for your boundary problem, you'll notice that you can accomplish some of the options yourself and others require you to ask someone else to make a change. Take a moment now to circle the options that you can accomplish on your own. I suggest you do this because if you can get what you need or want by changing your own behavior, it's often easier and more effective than trying to get someone else to change. Let's look at an example that highlights what's in your control and how changing yourself is sometimes the best option.

Lupe brought yogurt to work every day and put it in the communal refrigerator to eat as an afternoon snack. Repeatedly, when she went to get her yogurt, it was missing. Someone was eating her yogurt without permission—a clear boundary violation. One day, she saw Michelle eating yogurt just like her missing snack. Now, Lupe had several options for dealing with this boundary issue. She could ask Michelle to stop eating her yogurt. She would certainly be well within her rights to do so. But Michelle might refuse, or she might agree, but continue to eat the yogurt anyway. Lupe can't control what Michelle does. She can, however, change her own behavior. She could store her yogurt in an insulated lunch bag at her desk or bring another snack that doesn't require refrigeration.

Sometimes we resist the simplest solutions to our boundary issues—changing ourselves—because we're hurt or angry and think someone else should change. And perhaps Michelle *should* change; she's violating Lupe's boundaries and treating her poorly. But getting hung up on what we think others should do limits our options.

This isn't to say that Lupe shouldn't assert her needs and ask Michelle to stop eating her yogurt. That is a reasonable approach and in chapter 5 we'll focus on how to make such requests using assertive communication skills. The point here is that we give away our power when we allow others to dictate whether we can meet our needs. Often, changing ourselves is a valid option. And it's easier to do this when we replace the thought "I have to…" with "I choose to…" (Rosenberg 2003). When Lupe thinks *I choose to eat an apple* rather than *I have to eat an apple because Michelle keeps eating my yogurt*, she feels empowered, not victimized.

Assuming nothing else changes, how can *you* meet your unmet needs? How can *you* create the feelings you want to have? *Tip:* If you get stuck, look at your brainstormed list, particularly the items that are in your control.

Example: I can stop hanging out with Rachel, get together less frequently, only get together with Rachel when I have plenty of free time, not go to anything with a firm start time, tell Rachel to arrive thirty minutes before the actual start time, arrive late myself, leave if she's more than fifteen minutes late, start without her and stick to a firm end time, or do nothing and accept that Rachel will be late.

_____

_____

_____

_____

_____

What behavior change can someone else make that will meet your unmet needs and help you create the feelings you want to have?

Example: If Rachel arrives on time, I'll feel respected, at ease, and valued.

_____

_____

_____

Considering *all* the options that you've identified, which boundary makes the most sense for you to set? Remember, this is just a starting place; boundaries are flexible and can be changed if they don't effectively meet your needs.

Example: I'll only make plans with Rachel when I'm not in a rush and have time to allow for her to be late. And I won't make plans to do anything with a firm start time, like going to the movies.

_____

_____

_____

Why did you choose this option?

Example: It's in my control to make these changes. I've already talked to Rachel about being late several times and nothing has changed.

_____

_____

Once you've decided which boundaries will help you meet your needs and create positive feelings, you're ready to put them into action.

Step 3: Implement Your Boundaries

Use the following questions to plan how and when you'll implement your new boundaries. Some of the action items in your plan may be difficult or unpleasant and you might consciously or unconsciously avoid them. Creating a specific plan and time line will help you be accountable and increase the likelihood of carrying out your plan.

What will you do to set this boundary? Describe the actions that you'll take and the words that you'll use to communicate your boundary to others. Be as specific as possible.

Example: If Rachel invites me to get together when I have limited time or to go to an activity with a fixed start time, I'll say, "Unfortunately, that day (or activity) doesn't work for me. How about getting together on _____ (alternate date) to do _____ (alternate activity) instead?"

_____

_____

_____

_____

_____

When will you do this? (Include date and time, if possible.)

_____

_____

What action or change, if any, do you need to request from someone else? *Tip:* Be sure to use the strategies in chapter 5 to effectively make your requests.

_____

_____

_____

_____

_____

When will you make this request?

_____

_____

What will you do if others resist, ignore, or respond with anger to your boundary? Again, be as specific as possible and include what, how, and when you'll say or do something. Also, see chapters 5 and 6 for more information on dealing with resistance and boundary violations.

Example: If Rachel insists that we go to the movies, I'll say, "It sounds like a great movie, but I end up feeling annoyed when you're late and we miss the beginning of the movie. So, I don't think going to the movies is the best activity for us. How about going for a hike? Or we could watch a movie at my place together."

_____

_____

_____

_____

How will you know whether your boundary is effective? *Tip:* Review your desired outcome from Step 1.

Example: If my boundary is effective, I won't feel disrespected and annoyed. I'll feel at ease and valued when I spend time with Rachel.

_____

_____

_____

When do you think you'll know whether your boundaries are effective?

_____

What obstacles, if any, do you anticipate?

_____

_____

_____

_____

_____

Who or what might help you get past these obstacles?

_____

_____

_____

_____

_____

After you've implemented your plan, step 4 will help you adjust and improve your boundaries.

Step 4: Fine-Tune Your Boundaries

Boundaries are always a work in progress and we rarely create just the right boundary on the first attempt. So, try not to be disappointed if your boundaries don't initially achieve what you'd hoped or there are unforeseen challenges. It's normal to need to adjust your boundaries repeatedly. With practice, you'll get more skilled at identifying your needs and creating and implementing boundaries that meet your needs. But even then, you'll find that setting boundaries is more of an art than a science—and most will need adjusting.

WAS YOUR BOUNDARY SUCCESSFUL?

How will you know whether your new boundaries are successful? Since setting boundaries usually requires repetition before we completely achieve our desired results, it's helpful to look at what worked and what didn't work before we start making adjustments. And success is rarely all-or-nothing. So, even if you haven't completely achieved your desired outcome, I encourage you to notice small steps in the right direction. This can help you stay motivated and assess whether you're on the right track.

What boundary did you try to set?

_____

_____

What worked about this boundary?

_____

_____

What didn't work about this boundary?

_____

_____

What needs were you trying to meet with this boundary?

_____

Were your needs met? Rate how fully these needs were met on a scale of 1 to 10.

0   1   2   3   4   5   6   7   8   9   10

What positive feelings did you hope to have as a result of creating this boundary?

_____

Did your boundary help create positive feelings? On a scale of 1 to 10, rate how strongly you had the desired feelings. Remember, you aren't rating how you felt while setting the boundary, but how you felt in the same situation or with the same person after setting your boundary.

0   1   2   3   4   5   6   7   8   9   10

Overall, are you satisfied with this boundary? Did it meet enough of your needs and create enough of the feelings you hoped for?

_____

_____

_____

_____

_____

If yes, what is your plan for continuing to set this boundary? Be specific and include when and how you will do it.

_____

_____

_____

_____

_____

If you're not satisfied with the boundary you set, or if it didn't end up meeting all of your needs, keep reading. The rest of this chapter will help you make your boundaries more effective.

BOUNDARY PITFALLS

Our efforts to set boundaries can fall short for many different reasons. Let's look at some of the most common pitfalls: not following through with your plan, misidentifying your needs and feelings, not getting cooperation from another person, and giving up too soon.

Not following through. Like most things in life, if we don't follow through with our plan to set a boundary, we're not going to get the results we want. So, the first question to ask yourself is whether you implemented your plan fully. And if not, you want to understand what got in your way, so you can figure out how to overcome this barrier.

What did you do toward setting your boundary?

_____

_____

_____

_____

What part of your plan didn't you follow through on?

_____

_____

_____

_____

_____

What got in your way? Was it fear or false beliefs about boundaries? Or was it a lack of planning or a poor response from someone?

_____

_____

_____

_____

_____

Misidentifying your needs and feelings. Another common pitfall is misidentifying our needs and feelings. When this happens, we tend to feel dissatisfied with the outcome, but we're not sure why; we're following through, getting cooperation, and we've set the boundary multiple times, but we still feel disappointed by the results. Since a boundary is intended to meet a specific need or needs, if we identify the wrong need or only one of our needs, our boundary may not accomplish what we intended.

Let's revisit the example of my friend Rachel, who is chronically late. I initially identified a need for respect, which seemed reasonable because I felt disrespected and annoyed when she was late. However, I could've had other unmet needs, such as a need for connection or understanding. And if I met my need for respect by spending less time with Rachel, I wouldn't have met my need for connection or understanding. In this case, I may need a different boundary plan.

Do you have different or additional unmet needs that you didn't identify earlier?

_____

_____

Not getting cooperation from another person. You will also need to adjust your boundary if you asked someone else to make a change and they refused or didn't follow through with an agreed-upon change. Here, you'll need to decide whether to ask again or whether you can meet this need yourself.

First, make sure that you communicated what you need or want in a clear and respectful manner that was understood by the other person. If you didn't, it probably makes sense to adjust your approach and try again.

Was your request specific and clear? Did you communicate it respectfully and calmly? If not, how can you improve your request?

_____

_____

_____

If you communicated your boundary clearly and it wasn't respected, go back to your brainstorming list and see if you can create a new boundary plan that is within your control. For example, if I told Rachel that I feel disrespected when she's late and that I'd like her to arrive on time, but she continued to be late, I might create a new boundary by seeing Rachel less often (which is in my control and the natural consequence of her continuing to be late).

Is there a way for you to meet your need(s) yourself? How?

_____

_____

Giving up too soon. Sometimes we don't get the results we're looking for because we give up too soon. We'll rarely set a boundary once, get the result we want, and never have to revisit the issue. Setting boundaries is an ongoing process. Depending on the nature and duration of the problem, and the other people involved, we may need to set the same boundary multiple times.

It's natural to become frustrated and want to quit when our boundaries aren't successful—when the results don't match our expectations. This is why it's important to have realistic expectations about how much time and energy it takes to change our own behavior, our ability to change or influence other people's behavior, and other people's ability and motivation to change themselves. In most cases, we underestimate how difficult it is to change ourselves and we overestimate our ability to change others.

While boundaries require persistence, we also don't want to keep setting the same boundaries in the same ways if they're not working. Again, this will lead to frustration. Unfortunately, there isn't a set formula to tell us how many times we should set a boundary before deciding that it's not working and we should try something else. However, the following questions will help you gain some insight into what's right for you.

How many times have you tried to set this boundary using steps 1 through 3?

_____

How long has this boundary issue been a problem? (Usually, the longer the problem has existed, the longer it will take to change.)

_____

Have you seen any improvement? Change isn't all-or-nothing, and in some situations, even a small improvement can be a sign that you're on the right track and should stay the course. You may also find that a modest improvement (like Rachel being ten minutes late instead of twenty) meets enough of your needs to resolve the issue.

_____

_____

_____

Do you think you've given this boundary enough time and effort to work? Why or why not?

_____

_____

_____

How do you feel about continuing to set this boundary in the same way?

_____

_____

How do you feel about trying to set it differently?

_____

_____

Think about your answers to the questions above. Reflect on them for a day or two. After giving it some thought, does it make more sense to stick with your current plan or to make a different one?

_____

_____

CREATING A NEW PLAN

Once you have a better idea of why your boundaries aren't as successful as you'd like, you can fine-tune your original plan. Based on the pitfalls that you identified, choose one or more of the following adjustments.

- ☐ I will improve my follow-through by:

  - ☐ Getting support and/or accountability from _____ (specific people)

  - ☐ Committing to do _____ (specific action) on _____ (specific day/time)

  - ☐ Other _____

- ☐ I will create a new boundary plan based on the additional need(s) I identified.

- ☐ I will improve how I communicate my boundary by:

  - ☐ Being more specific about what I need or want

  - ☐ Being polite and respectful

  - ☐ Making sure the other person hears and understands me

  - ☐ Staying calm

  - ☐ Using I-statements

  - ☐ Other _____

☐   I will create a new boundary plan based on things I can do rather than relying on someone else to change.

☐   I will stick with my original plan and set this boundary at least _____ more times.

You should now have a list of actionable ways to adjust and improve your boundaries. However, if you still don't get the results you want or you feel increasingly frustrated, return to step 4 to continue to fine-tune your boundary. It's not unusual to repeat step 4 multiple times.

For easy reference, a condensed version of the Four Steps to Setting Better Boundaries can be found in the Appendix and at http://www.newharbinger.com/47582.

Summary

In this chapter, you learned a four-step formula for setting boundaries that meet your needs and replace negative feelings with positive ones. We also discussed how to set boundaries by changing our own behavior or by asking someone else to change their behavior. The next chapter will focus on how to assertively communicate your boundaries to others, which will strengthen your relationships and increase the likelihood that others will understand and respect your boundaries.

Chapter 5

Communicating Your Boundaries

Communicating your boundaries can be challenging and scary, especially if it hasn't gone well in the past. As a result, many of us avoid asking for what we want and need, or we make demands and lash out in anger. Neither approach helps us meet our needs or create the trusting, respectful relationships that we crave. In this chapter, you'll learn how to effectively communicate your boundaries using assertive communication skills, which will increase the chances of your needs being met, decrease anger and frustration, and create goodwill.

Components of Effective Communication

Effective communication is a skill that everyone can learn. However, if you've never been taught or had the chance to practice communication skills, it's a bit like learning a foreign language. At first, it feels awkward and takes a lot of effort. But with practice, assertive communication gets easier and feels more natural, and you'll begin to see positive results in your relationships. In the next section, we'll review the components of effective communication and start practicing them.

Be Assertive

There are three basic types of communication: passive, aggressive, and assertive. When we're passive, we don't demonstrate self-respect because we aren't speaking up about what we need or being honest about how we feel; we minimize our needs and feelings to please or appease others. When we're aggressive, we don't respect other people's needs and feelings; we're harsh, hurtful, and demanding, believing that our needs and feeling supersede others'. But when we're assertive, we convey our needs and feelings clearly and directly, in a way that respects ourselves and others.

Make Requests, Not Demands

If your boundary involves asking someone else to make a change or take an action, you'll want to make a request, not a demand. Demands create defensiveness and resistance rather than cooperation. Using *I-statements* and being willing to compromise are two ways you can make more effective requests.

I-STATEMENTS

It's normal to feel angry or frustrated when your needs aren't being met. For many, this leads to blaming, put-downs, and demands. It might sound something like this: "I need you to stop being so loud. You're so inconsiderate!" Not surprisingly, this approach doesn't create understanding and cooperation. It usually results in defensiveness; others dig in their heels and put their energy into proving you wrong rather than understanding your needs and working with you to find a solution.

An "I-statement" uses a set formula (see below) to communicate how you feel and what you want. I-statements work well because when you focus on how you feel, not on how egregious the other person's behavior is, you're likely to build empathy rather than defensiveness.

Sometimes, people aren't aware of how their behavior negatively affects others, but when we let them know they're hurting us, they're more willing to change or compromise. I-statements are a tool that can help others understand your experiences and needs, and, as a result, be open to finding a solution.

Here's the basic formula for an I-statement:

I feel _____ when/that _____

and I'd like _____.

Example: I feel frustrated when you don't tell me that you're coming home late, and I'd like you to text me if you're going to be home later than 6:30.

To improve your I-statement, you can directly ask for the other person's agreement.

Example: I feel frustrated when you don't tell me that you're coming home late, and I'd like you to text me if you're going to be home later than 6:30. Is that something you're willing to do?

If the other person agrees, you now have a clear agreement about what they will do differently. And if they don't agree, you can either work toward a compromise or, if that's not possible, take other actions to meet your needs and take care of yourself.

Before we discuss how to compromise, practice completing the I-statement formula to communicate a boundary.

I feel _____ when/that _____

and I'd like _____.

Is that something you're willing to do?

"IT WOULD MEAN A LOT"

Not all requests are equally important, so when your request is important, you should communicate this. In *The Assertiveness Guide for Women*, Julie Hanks (2016) suggests using the phrase "It would mean a lot to me if..." She explains that this phrase is effective because "it starts with owning that this request is *you* wanting it—that it is meaningful to *you*...This makes it more likely that the other person will remain open to hearing your request and won't shut down or become defensive" (173). This phrase helps the recipient differentiate it from less important issues or requests—and hopefully take it more seriously.

Variations of this phrase include:

- This is really important to me.

- I would appreciate it if...

- I have a request that means a lot to me.

- I'm very concerned about this.

Be Specific

Requests are most effective when they're specific. Usually, we *think* we're being clear and specific because we know what we want. And when we assume that the other person is on the same page, we may not give enough detail about what we're requesting.

Another common problem is that we haven't clarified for ourselves what we're asking for. You may have a general idea, such as *I want to be treated with respect*, but you haven't identified what specifically you want the other person to do differently. Notice the difference between these three requests:

I'd like you to treat me with respect.

Please don't call or text me late at night.

Please don't call or text me after 10 p.m.

Which request is going to help the listener best understand what you want and most likely get the result that you're looking for? The third example is the most effective because it identifies a specific behavior and time, which helps the listener understand exactly what you want. This decreases misunderstandings and allows the listener to accurately evaluate whether they're willing to change the behavior.

Tips for being specific:

- Whenever possible, identify an observable action that you want someone to make.
- Quantify how often, how much, or for how long you want the new behavior to last.
- Give specific times and dates.
- Give an example of what you're requesting.

See if you can rewrite the following boundary requests so they're more specific.

I feel frustrated that you left a mess. I'd like you to clean up after yourself.

_____

Please don't give my kids so much junk food.

_____

Try writing a boundary request of your own, being as specific as possible.

_____

Be Confident

Setting limits and making requests are also more effective when you can deliver your message confidently, knowing that you have the right to do so, that your feelings and needs matter, and that you're capable of solving your problems.

> **Tip** Don't undermine your requests with terms such as:
>
> Sort of
>
> Kind of
>
> Maybe
>
> Just

Confidence doesn't mean cockiness, which has an air of superiority. Confidence shows that you believe in what you're saying, and you can state what you need or want without apologizing, overexplaining, or needing to justify it. Apologizing and justifying can water down requests, suggesting they aren't important or that you shouldn't ask for what you need.

Notice the difference between these requests:

I'm really sorry to bother you. If it's not too much trouble, I wanted to ask you not to park in front of my driveway. I don't mean to be difficult. It's just that when I get parked in, I'm late for work and my boss is a real stickler for time.

Hi, Joe. Your car is blocking my driveway. Can you please park somewhere else?

The second example is straightforward, but still polite and respectful. I have the right to get in and out of my driveway and don't need to justify or apologize for my request.

Assertive communication can feel uncomfortable or seem harsh if you've been overapologizing and justifying your boundaries, but a warm tone of voice can go a long way in delivering your message effectively and will make assertive communication feel more authentic.

Check for Understanding

We can also avoid misunderstandings by checking for understanding. Simply ask, *Does this make sense?* or *Is this clear?* or *Do you have any questions?*

Therapists use a technique called reflective listening, which is more involved and can feel quite stilted at first, but it's effective. It works like this. After you've made your request, the other person paraphrases what you said using their own words and then asks you, *Did I get that right? Did I leave anything out?* You then tell them whether they accurately conveyed all that you said or, if not, gently tell them what was omitted or incorrect. The other person tries again to accurately describe what you said. This is repeated until you feel that you've been understood.

You can also look for nonverbal signs that the other person has been listening to you, such as eye contact and nodding. Although these don't always translate into understanding, attention and listening are good signs that your conversation is on track.

Be Consistent

When setting boundaries, we must be consistent and firm, especially with those who resist our boundaries. Some may push back by arguing or using passive-aggressive behavior (like pretending not to hear you) in hopes that you'll back down. It's important to stick to your boundaries, especially if you're sure you've been heard and understood. You may need to repeat your boundaries multiple times before some people realize that you're serious about your boundaries and will follow through with consequences.

Notice Your Tone of Voice

It's not just what we say, but *how* we say it that matters. Your tone of voice can completely change the meaning of what you say. When setting boundaries, aim for a pleasant but firm tone of voice that conveys confidence and a receptive attitude. Yelling may feel empowering or even necessary with people who talk over you or raise their voices. But, again, yelling doesn't encourage listening and cooperation. Often, people tune out yelling, sarcasm, or a harsh tone of voice because it feels critical or hurtful. A pleasant but firm voice is more effective.

Choose the Right Time

Timing matters when communicating our boundaries. It's tempting to say things in the moment when we feel an urgency about the issue or are flooded with emotion. But when we respond impulsively, we're more likely to be harsh and say things we regret. So, unless someone is in immediate danger, it's often better to wait until you've collected your thoughts, processed your feelings, and had time to clarify your needs and boundaries.

Ideally, choose a time when you're both calm, sober, well rested, and not distracted by the television, phone, other people, or problems. Realistically, there isn't a perfect time to discuss boundaries and if you wait too long, you run the risk of having resentments pile up. So, choose the best possible time. For some busy couples or families, it works well to routinely schedule time to check in and discuss issues such as needs, schedules, and relationship issues, including boundaries.

More and more of our communication takes place via text message. While it's convenient, it isn't effective for more complex or emotionally laden conversations. When we're texting, we lose body language and tone of voice cues, and we're often distracted or multitasking too, which makes misunderstandings more likely. So, if you anticipate that a boundary conversation will be difficult or you started a conversation by text and it's not going well, plan a time to talk in person. Even though it may feel uncomfortable to talk face-to-face, you'll probably get better results. And if in person isn't possible, a video or regular call is still an improvement over texting; it allows you to pay more attention to valuable nuances of speech and tone.

Calm Yourself

Setting boundaries can bring up challenging emotions. Being aware of how you feel, whether it's fearful, angry, or worried, will help you regain your emotional equilibrium, which will, in turn, help you communicate your boundaries effectively. Before setting a boundary, take a brief time-out to notice your thoughts and how you're feeling; perhaps even write them down. Notice how your body feels. Is it tense? Is your heart racing? Are you sweating? If so, try one of the following activities to soothe yourself before having a conversation.

GROUNDING

Grounding is a quick and easy way to calm yourself. It uses mindfulness principles to refocus your attention on concrete, observable sensations. It *grounds* you in the present, so you aren't ruminating about the past or worrying about the future. Try the following example of mental grounding.

To begin, rate your stress or anxiety on a scale of 1 to 10.   _____

Take a few slow, deep breaths. Then, ask yourself the following questions.

Name five things you can see.

_____

_____

_____

How many electrical outlets are in this room?   _____

What does the chair or couch you're sitting on feel like? Is it soft? Rough? Smooth?

_____

How many green items can you see?   _____

What do you smell?

_____

Describe the shoes you're wearing in as much detail as possible.

_____

_____

Name three sounds you hear.

_____

Pick up a nearby object. What does it feel like? How much does it weigh?

_____

_____

Rerate your anxiety on a scale of 1 to 10.   _____

If it is over a 5, repeat the grounding exercise.

In the future, you can do this exercise mentally, without writing down your answers.

You can also try a physical grounding exercise. Again, begin and end by rating your anxiety level. But this time refocus your thoughts and feelings via a physical sensation, such as sticking your hand in a bowl of ice water or holding an ice cube and noticing how it feels.

MANTRAS

A mantra is a positive statement that you repeat to yourself to help motivate, encourage, or calm yourself. Read the following examples and then try writing your own:

I've got this.

I'm calm and confident.

I can handle whatever happens.

It's okay to ask for what I need.

_____

_____

_____

_____

_____

OTHER WAYS TO SELF-SOOTHE

Circle the strategies you will try and use the blank spaces to list other ideas. Here are some examples:

- Go for a walk.
- Take a bath or shower.
- Write down your thoughts and feelings.
- Listen to calming music.
- Stretch.
- Rub your shoulders and neck.
- Box breathing—inhale for a count of 4, hold your breath for a count of 4, exhale for a count of 4; repeat for 1 to 2 minutes.

- Place your hand over your heart; notice your chest rising and falling with each breath. Expand your chest as much as you can with each inhale. As you exhale, visualize tension flowing out like air leaving a deflating balloon.

- Think of ten things you're grateful for.

- Pet your cat or dog.

- _____

- _____

- _____

Phew! We've gone over a lot of communication skills—and it can be a lot to take in. Don't expect that you'll remember them all or execute them perfectly. The most important thing is that you keep working at them. Your skills will improve the more you use them!

Compromise and Nonnegotiable Boundaries

When we compromise, we consider other people's needs as well as our own. And because it's mutual, compromise builds positive feelings in a relationship and usually leaves both parties feeling satisfied. But compromise can be challenging!

Of course, you can't make someone compromise if they don't want to, but you can communicate in a way that encourages compromise. Using an I-statement is a good start, but you also need to be willing to hear the other person's point of view and consider alternate solutions. Here's an example of how a simple boundary negotiation might go.

Me: I feel frustrated when you don't tell me that you're coming home late, and I'd like you to text me if you're going to be home later than 6:30. Is that something you're willing to do?

Husband: I'm willing to do that, but I get so wrapped up in work that I might forget. Could you call me at 6:00 and ask what time I'll be home?

Me: No, I'm busy helping the kids with homework and cooking dinner at 6:00. Could you set an alarm to remind yourself to text me by 6:30?

Husband: Sure. I can do that.

This was an easy negotiation because it's a low-stakes issue; neither of us felt very strongly about it or were especially attached to one particular solution. However, when we're negotiating important issues (such as safety or health concerns) or have strong emotional responses, reaching a compromise is more challenging.

Identifying Nonnegotiable Boundaries

We all have nonnegotiable boundaries, things we aren't willing to compromise about—and that's okay. Just make sure that you don't categorize too many boundaries as deal breakers because then you're probably becoming too rigid with your boundaries or you're making idle threats, both of which can be counterproductive. Aim to identify just four or five nonnegotiable boundaries that you need in your life right now. Here are some examples:

- I don't allow peanut products in my home because my daughter has a severe peanut allergy.

- I won't be in the same room as my stepmother due to her abusive behavior.

- Smoking is not allowed in my house.

- Guns must always be locked in a gun safe.

What are your nonnegotiable boundaries?

_____

_____

_____

_____

_____

Now that you know what your nonnegotiable boundaries are, you can try to be flexible and open to compromise on your other boundaries. Compromise is usually good for both parties, but be careful about being too accommodating. Many people who struggle with boundaries confuse compromising and conceding. Conceding is one party giving in or giving up, whereas compromising involves give and take by both parties. When it's truly mutual, compromising feels good, or at least productive. But if you frequently make significant concessions because you're afraid of conflict or don't feel confident asserting your needs while the other person doesn't budge, then your needs won't get met and you'll grow resentful.

How will you know if you're conceding rather than compromising? Often, your thoughts, feelings, and bodily sensations will let you know when you've made a concession, rather than a true compromise. You might feel out of sorts or disappointed; you might experience a sneaking sense that you've been taken advantage of.

Describe how you've felt in the past when you know you've conceded, how the other person treated you, and how your body reacted.

_____

_____

_____

_____

_____

If achieving true compromise in your relationships is difficult, here is some additional language you can use:

- How can we work together to get both of our needs met?

- I'd like to find a solution that will work for both of us.

- If we're both willing to give a bit, I'm sure we can reach an agreement.

- I think we have the same goal. We just need to hammer out the details.

- What would work for you?

  I need _____ from you. What do you need from me?

- Can we try it this way and then if it doesn't work for you, we'll renegotiate?

- I'd like to hear what you think.

  I need _____, but I'm open to hearing your ideas about how I can get/do this in a way that will work for you, too.

Preparing for difficult conversations can also help you navigate these discussions more successfully and easily.

Practice and Preparation for Effective Boundary Setting

Communication skills are complex and take a lot of practice to master. It's normal to feel anxious about setting boundaries, having difficult conversations, and using new skills. Following are tips and techniques for practicing assertive communication and preparing for difficult conversations.

Write a Script

One of the most effective ways to practice setting boundaries is to write a script or an outline of what you want to say and how you'll say it. You can also include how you anticipate the other person will respond. You don't have to follow the script exactly, but the process of writing it can increase your confidence, reduce anxious feelings, and help you troubleshoot potential problems.

Try writing a script for a difficult boundary that you need to set.

_____

_____

_____

_____

_____

Once you've written your script, read through it a couple of times. Read it out loud and make any necessary changes. You may want to practice it with a trusted friend or record yourself to see how it sounds.

Visualize Success

A related strategy is to visualize yourself successfully setting boundaries. To do this, find a quiet place and close your eyes if it feels comfortable. Imagine yourself using assertive communication skills to set a boundary that's been difficult for you. Where are you? Who are you with? What are you saying and doing? What is your tone of voice? How does it feel?

You can also describe your visualization here.

_____

_____

_____

_____

_____

Practice with "Safe" People

When you're learning to set boundaries, don't start with the most difficult people in your life. Instead, start with people who are "safe," meaning they're generally agreeable, respectful, and interested in your well-being, and you have the sense that they'll respond favorably to your requests. Starting with safe people will most likely lead to successful boundary setting and negotiating, which will boost your confidence and motivation. As you grow more skilled at setting boundaries, you can work toward setting boundaries with the more challenging people in your life.

Who are some safe people that you can practice setting boundaries with?

_____

_____

_____

_____

_____

Notice How Others Set Boundaries

We can learn a lot by watching how other people set boundaries, noticing what works and doesn't work, and what we would do the same or differently. Over the next several weeks, pay attention to how people set boundaries at your place of employment, worship, or the grocery store: how they ask for what they need or let others know what is or isn't okay with them, what tone of voice or word choices are effective, and so forth.

What did you learn by watching how others set boundaries? How can this information help you improve your boundary-setting skills?

_____

_____

_____

_____

_____

Reinforce Positive Responses

One of the basic tenets of behavioral psychology is that people learn and are motivated by positive reinforcement, meaning that if you respond positively to someone's behavior, it's more likely that this behavior will be repeated. So, when someone responds favorably to your limits or requests, be sure to let them know. You can do this with a smile or warm facial expression, saying something like, *I really appreciate that you took the time to listen to me* or *I know this is hard and I'm glad we're able to work together on a solution*, or spending time with them. The form of positive reinforcement that you choose will vary depending on the circumstances and people involved.

What are some positive reinforcements that you might use when setting boundaries?

_____

_____

_____

_____

_____

Give People Time to Adjust

If you're beginning to set boundaries after years of letting things go or saying yes to every request, it can come as a shock to those around you. They may be confused or angered by your new behavior, especially if you haven't told them that you're working on setting boundaries. There are probably a few people in your life who resist attempts to set boundaries, but most people will be supportive if you help them understand why you're setting boundaries and give them time to adjust.

Here's an example of how Joy handled this with her sister Gabby.

Joy: I want to let you know that I'm trying to set healthier boundaries. I'm not going to lend Mom any more money and, starting next month, I can't babysit for you on Mondays. I'm not upset with you. This is something I need to do for myself.

Gabby: Really? It sounds like you're abandoning me!

Joy: That's not my intention. I'm constantly exhausted and anxious. I'm in debt and I don't have time to spend with my own kids. It's not healthy to go on like this. I need to learn how to say no.

Gabby: Yeah, I get it. Mom has no boundaries…And I guess mine aren't so great either.

Joy: I know it's an adjustment. That's why I want to tell you.

Who would it be helpful to tell that you're learning to set better boundaries?

_____

_____

_____

What will you tell them about why or how you're changing?

_____

_____

_____

If you're nervous, consider writing a script to practice this conversation.

_____

_____

_____

_____

_____

_____

_____

Learn to Say No

Saying no is notoriously guilt-provoking and many of us avoid it because it seems harsh or selfish. We don't want to hurt people's feelings or be difficult; we don't want to disappoint or anger others. We want to be helpful and agreeable, so we say yes (or nothing) when we really want to say no. This is completely understandable! But saying no is an essential part of setting boundaries. It's how we protect ourselves from unwanted touch and from committing to things we don't have time for. It's the most basic way we assert our needs and independence. So, let's talk about how you can say no in the nicest way possible and still be clear and unwavering.

"I Have a Policy"

Patti Breitman and Connie Hatch, authors of the book *How to Say No Without Feeling Guilty* (2001), suggest using the phrase "I have a policy." It goes something like this:

Kris: Hey, George. My truck's in the shop. Could I borrow your car tomorrow?

George: Sorry, I have a policy about not lending my car.

According to Breitman and Hatch, "I have a policy" makes your refusal feel less personal because you're saying no on general principle not based on this specific request or person. It also conveys that you've given this issue enough thought to have established a policy about it.

Of course, policies shouldn't be random excuses that you throw together when you feel under pressure. If you're going to make policies about not lending expensive items to friends, not drinking alcohol on weeknights, or anything else, make sure they're thought out and reflect your priorities.

What are your priorities? They could be cultivating strong family relationships, staying physically healthy, or saving money.

_____

_____

_____

_____

_____

What personal policies might help you safeguard your priorities?

_____

_____

_____

_____

_____

"Let Me Think About It"

Is yes your default answer when someone asks for your help or wants you to do something? Many of us blurt out yes without thinking it through. Very few situations require an immediate response, even though in our fast-paced, technology-driven lives, they can seem like they do. Even text messages are rarely urgent. Some people may want you to reply instantaneously, but it's usually not necessary. So, before you say yes to another commitment or favor, slow down. Take time to think about the request. Look at your calendar and review your priorities before deciding.

If you need to respond in the moment, tell the other person that you need time to consider your options, using one of these phrases:

- Let me think about it.

- I need to check my calendar.

- I'm not sure. I'll need to get back to you.

It's okay to postpone deciding so you can give it thoughtful consideration. But it's important to circle back and give a definitive answer, rather than letting the matter slide. If possible, let the other person know when you'll get back to them by saying something like:

- Can I let you know tomorrow?

- I'd like to talk it over with Marli. I'll call you Friday with my answer.

This approach will help the other person feel respected and valued, even if your answer is no.

Half-Truths and Lies

At times, it may be tempting to set a boundary with a "half-truth" or lie. To spare your friend's feelings, you might cancel plans for dinner, telling him that your child is sick rather than that you find his partner's political views unbearable. Or it may be easier to tell your boss that you were out of town and didn't have cell service than explain that you didn't want to talk to him on your day off.

Lies aren't necessarily wrong in every situation and, ultimately, it's up to you to decide whether you feel comfortable telling an occasional lie. However, be careful that you don't rely on lies to avoid difficult conversations—like setting boundaries. Lies can damage relationships, especially when they're exposed. Even if the truth is never revealed, lies can feel inauthentic and increase feelings of guilt.

Before using a lie to set a boundary, ask yourself these questions:

- Have I tried to be honest and direct about my needs? Why or why not?

- Is there a way for me to be honest, yet kind?

- Is this lie likely to damage a relationship?

- How do I feel about lying in this specific situation?

More Ways to Say No

- No thanks.
- That doesn't work for me.
- Thanks for thinking of me. I really wish I could.
- I'd love to, but I'm already overcommitted.
- Unfortunately, that's not something I can do at this time.
- I'm already booked.
- I'm not interested.
- Maybe next time.
- I wish I could, but I just can't.
- I don't think I'm the right person to help with that.
- I'm sorry I can't help you this time.
- That sounds fun, but I just can't afford it right now.
- It's not a good time.
- I can't take on any new projects.
- That sounds interesting, but it doesn't align with my priorities.
- I'm focused on my family right now, so I'm limiting my other commitments.
- That's not my strong suit, so I'm going to decline.

Sometimes, Actions Are Better Than Words

So far, we've focused on communicating boundaries verbally, but I also want to touch on how and when to communicate boundaries nonverbally. Words aren't always the best way to communicate your boundaries. Sometimes, you need to take action to protect yourself or others and an explanation isn't helpful or may make matters worse. For example, you might get up from the sofa and move across the room if your uncle, who's been sexually inappropriate with you, sits next to you. In this situation, you don't need to explain why you're moving—and doing so might lead to embarrassment or conflict that you'd rather avoid.

You might consider simply acting rather than explaining your needs or boundaries in these situations:

- You or someone else is being harmed (or at risk of being harmed).

- You're dealing with someone who's under the influence of drugs or alcohol.

- You're dealing with someone who's acting irrationally, dangerously, or erratically.

- You've previously explained your boundaries and this person repeatedly violates them.

- Explaining your needs or boundaries to this person is likely to lead to an argument or physical altercation, you'll be blamed or shamed, or your words will be used against you.

Is there a person or situation that you've encountered, or are likely to encounter, where it might be best to act on your boundaries rather than explain them? Write about what's happened or how you'll act to keep yourself safe, knowing what you know now about boundaries and how to establish them.

_____

_____

_____

_____

_____

In chapter 11, we'll discuss how to set boundaries with difficult people in more detail.

Summary

In this chapter you learned about how to communicate your boundaries using the components of effective communication, how to practice and prepare for setting your boundaries, how to say no, and that sometimes actions are more helpful than explanations. Communication skills are challenging, so continue to practice these skills and revisit this chapter for tune-ups. Next, we'll address how to handle boundary violations.

Chapter 6

Handling Boundary Violations

So far, you've learned how to identify your boundaries and communicate them to others. Unfortunately, there will be times when your boundaries are violated or disrespected. It's important to consider how to handle boundary violations, understand the importance of enforcing consequences, and explore how boundary violations impact our relationships.

What Is a Boundary Violation?

Have you ever tried to set a boundary only to be ignored or not taken seriously? Or perhaps you've had someone get angry when you set a limit, or they agreed to change their behavior but didn't follow through. These are examples of boundary violations—and they're painful experiences. The following examples provide a closer look at different kinds of boundary violations.

Mercedes reaches for a second helping of potatoes. Her mother glares at her and says, "Are you sure you want more potatoes? How about some salad instead?"

"No, I want potatoes, Mom," she replies.

"But aren't you worried about your figure? You look like you've put on a few pounds."

"Mom, we've had this conversation many times. I'm a grown woman and I'm capable of managing my weight. I'd like you to stop commenting on what I'm eating and how much I weigh."

"Oh, I didn't mean anything by it. You always take things the wrong way. You know I love you."

Bobbie rented Daniel a room in her house. Before he moved in, she explicitly laid out the expectation that he would clean the kitchen after he used it and she cautioned him about not putting too much toilet paper in the toilet because the plumbing was sensitive. He agreed. However, within the first week of his tenancy, he left dishes in the sink three times and clogged the toilet. So, Bobbie gently reminded Daniel of their agreement. But instead of an apology or taking responsibility for his actions, he yelled at her, "I have to work mandatory overtime! I'm exhausted! Don't you have any compassion?"

Can you relate to Mercedes or Bobbie? As you can see, some boundary violations are more passive, even camouflaged as care and concern like Mercedes's mother's, and other violations are overt and harsh.

What kinds of boundary violations have you experienced?

_____

_____

_____

_____

_____

How does it feel when your boundaries are violated? How does it affect your relationship with the other person?

_____

_____

_____

_____

_____

Boundary violations are inevitable, but that doesn't mean we can't do anything about them. So, let's think about how we can respond to get our needs met and preserve our relationships, if possible.

Responding to Boundary Violations

Figuring out how to address boundary violations isn't easy! In general, responding assertively, using the communications skills from chapter 5, is a good rule of thumb. If we're passive (and don't address boundary violations) or aggressive (responding with anger, demands, or ultimatums), we probably won't get what we want or need. However, there may be times that it makes sense to let a boundary violation go unaddressed. Let's explore how to figure out what kind of response will achieve your goals and meet your needs.

Think of a time when you weren't sure how to respond to a boundary violation or your response didn't lead to the results you wanted. Describe the situation and some of the ways you could have responded.

_____

_____

_____

_____

_____

Now, use the same situation to answer the following questions to get a better sense of the factors that influence how you respond.

Rate how important this issue is on a scale of 1 to 10. Why did you score it as you did? Is it a deal breaker? Is it a safety issue?

_____

_____

_____

_____

_____

How were you affected by the boundary violation? Rate the strength of your feelings from 1 to 10. Higher levels of negative emotions (such as anger, irritation, frustration, hopelessness, or sadness) are another indication that this is an important issue for you.

_____

_____

_____

_____

Understanding how important the boundary is and how you were affected by the violation will help you figure out whether to respond and in what way. Note that safety issues always need to be addressed, as you need to keep yourself and others safe.

How did you communicate your need or want in this situation? What did you say? What was your tone? Was your request clear and specific?

_____

_____

_____

_____

Were you heard? How do you know that you were understood?

_____

_____

_____

_____

If your boundary was violated because you didn't make a specific request or you weren't heard or understood, you might restate your boundary request before taking any other action.

What's the nature of your relationship with the person who violated your boundaries? Rate how important the relationship is from 1 to 10.

_____

_____

_____

_____

_____

Being aware of the nature and importance of the relationship will also help you decide how to respond. For example, when you have a meaningful relationship that you want to maintain you'll consider different options than you would with a stranger or someone you don't care to have a relationship with.

Has this happened before? Is there a pattern of boundary violations by this person? If so, what does the pattern tell you?

_____

_____

_____

_____

_____

If someone repeatedly disrespects your boundaries, it doesn't mean that you're doing it wrong or that you shouldn't set boundaries with this person. More likely, it means that you need to try a different approach to setting your boundary and increase your self-care to cope with this person. In chapter 11, we'll talk more about dealing with repeat boundary violators.

Now you can decide whether you should respond to this boundary violation and if so, how.

Does this boundary violation warrant a response? Why or why not?

_____

_____

_____

_____

_____

When we respond to a boundary violation, it's usually by enforcing a consequence, which is the focus of the next section.

Enforcing Consequences

A consequence is an action that you take in response to a boundary violation to protect yourself. It can be anything from leaving the room to filing for divorce.

Usually, people who struggle to set boundaries also struggle to enforce consequences. But what's the point of asking your wife to stop ridiculing you in public if you're going to sit idly by if she continues? Without consequences, boundaries become meaningless. We need to choose consequences that feel right to us and that we're willing to enforce.

CONSEQUENCES VS. PUNISHMENTS

Just as a boundary isn't intended to be a punishment, the consequence of crossing a boundary is also not a punishment. Remember, our boundaries serve to protect us. So, if one of our boundaries is crossed, we have to find a different way to protect ourselves. For example, if your spouse has an affair, you might distance yourself and take other steps to protect yourself—perhaps consulting an attorney or refusing to have unprotected sex with your spouse. Even though you'd probably feel angry and might even want to retaliate against your spouse, the purpose of a consequence is self-protection, not punishment. This is an important but potentially muddy distinction. The best way to know the difference is to ask yourself, *How will this consequence help me protect and take care of myself?*

At this point, you may be wondering, *What's wrong with punishing someone who's violated my boundaries and treated me poorly?* That's a valid question! Wanting to retaliate is understandable. Retaliating feels powerful; it feels like self-protection, but rarely is. Often, retaliating puts you in more danger because it keeps the conflict going. Thus, you fail to resolve the original issue *and* you create more distance and animosity in your relationships. Conversely, enforcing consequences is assertive; you're standing up for yourself in a way that respects you and the other person.

Using the same boundary violation that you identified in the previous exercise (or a different one, if you concluded no response was warranted), what consequences make sense and seem enforceable to you?

_____

_____

_____

_____

_____

Now that you've identified some consequences, let's focus on *how* to enforce them.

HOW TO ENFORCE CONSEQUENCES

Having your boundaries crossed is likely to stir up strong feelings. We don't make the best decisions when we're angry, hurt, or embarrassed. So, take some time to think through your options and use the strategies in chapter 5 to self-soothe and reduce the intensity of your feelings before speaking or acting. Again, you don't want to give an ultimatum or make threats that you don't intend to follow through on.

Depending on the situation, you may or may not want to verbally state the consequence. Emma's and Maya's stories provide examples of both approaches.

Emma was angry and hurt when she discovered her boyfriend was having an affair. She wanted to salvage her relationship and she also knew that she needed to set boundaries to take care of herself. She told her boyfriend that to rebuild safety and trust in their relationships, he needed to cut off all contact with the other woman—and if he didn't, Emma would leave and go stay with her mother.

Maya immediately hit it off with her new coworker Angela. They started eating lunch together several times a week and had fun talking about reality shows they both watched. But when Maya shared that she was dating a much older woman, Angela was critical. And she persisted in criticizing Maya's partner nearly every time they had lunch together. Maya was hurt and pulled away. She started working through lunch or made plans with other coworkers, making herself less available to spend time with Angela.

Emma opted to tell her boyfriend about the consequence before she acted, while Maya chose to enforce the consequence without saying anything to Angela. Neither approach is inherently right or wrong. For Emma, given the importance of the relationship with her boyfriend, her desire to rebuild trust and safety, and the severity of the consequence, she thought it was appropriate to inform him of the consequence before she enforced it. However, if she thought her boyfriend would become physically aggressive or manipulative if she told him, it would've been safer to go to her mother's without explanation. And even though Maya was hurt by Angela's behavior, they didn't have a close or long-term relationship that Maya was invested in continuing. If you're unsure about whether to explain or state a consequence, consider the following aspects of the situation:

- Whether it's safer to explain the consequence or not

- The nature and importance of the relationship

- The severity of the boundary violation or the intended consequence

- Whether there's a pattern of boundary violations by this person that indicates they're unlikely to change

Look back at Mercedes's and Bobbie's stories at the beginning of this chapter and consider how you'd enforce consequences in each situation. Again, there isn't a right or wrong answer; the purpose of this exercise is for you to think about the pros and cons of different approaches and settle on what feels right to you.

What would you do if you were Mercedes?

_____

_____

_____

_____

_____

What would you do if you were Bobbie?

_____

_____

_____

_____

_____

What was it about Mercedes's and Bobbie's situations that led you to enforce consequences similarly or differently?

_____

_____

_____

_____

_____

Difficult Choices

Sometimes, boundary violations force us to make difficult choices. Sometimes, we have a lot to lose by enforcing the consequences of a boundary violation. For example, it's easy to say that you'd leave your spouse if they cheated on you, but the reality of what you might lose—financial security, your home, supportive in-laws, your children's stability—may make leaving extremely difficult.

In some situations, we can accept that our needs aren't fully met. But some boundaries are deal breakers and absolutely must be maintained if we're going to continue to have a relationship with someone or allow them into our homes or to be around our children. But even the consequences of deal breakers can be hard to enforce when there's a lot at stake. And yet, the cost of doing nothing can be even higher. When we allow people to violate our deal breaker boundaries, we pay with our self-respect, safety, health, and self-esteem (and sometimes our children's health and well-being, too). The following stories are examples of difficult choices that some of us face.

> *Roger and Judy's daughter Sara, thirty-two, became addicted to painkillers after a car accident when she was eighteen years old. Since then, she's struggled—she's been homeless and used heroin between stints in jail and rehab. Roger and Judy never stopped worrying about Sara. So, when she showed up six months pregnant, they welcomed her home and helped her get sober. But soon after her daughter was born, she relapsed. She continued to use drugs, coming and going at all hours, stealing, and verbally abusing her parents. Roger and Judy desperately want to set boundaries, to tell Sara that her behavior is unacceptable and she needs to leave. But every time they try, Sara threatens to take her daughter and never return. Roger and Judy have raised their granddaughter for the past three years and they can't bear the thought of Sara taking her.*

> *Nori has a job that she loves, with great pay and benefits, and opportunities to advance. Her manager has been making unwanted sexual advances that make her uncomfortable. She's tried to address it with him, but he brushes off her concerns. She feels anxious, finds it hard to concentrate, and has insomnia. Nori has considered telling her manager's boss, but she's afraid of the repercussions. She could get fired or blackballed in her field. She's also considered quitting, but she needs the money to help support her parents and doesn't think she can find another job that pays as well.*

Do you identify with Roger and Judy's or Nori's dilemmas? Even if the details of your difficult choices are different, you can use the following questions to help sort through your thoughts, feelings, and options.

What boundary violation presents a difficult choice for you?

_____

_____

_____

_____

_____

How have you or others been hurt by this boundary violation?

_____

_____

_____

_____

_____

What keeps you from enforcing the consequences of this boundary violation? What might you lose if you enforce your boundaries?

_____

_____

_____

_____

_____

What might you gain?

_____

_____

_____

_____

_____

How do you feel when you think about what you've already lost versus what you might gain?

_____

_____

_____

_____

_____

These questions may bring up some overwhelming or upsetting feelings, so let's pause here. This section is called *Difficult Choices* because the choices these boundary violations ask you to make are truly difficult, often life-altering decisions. And I don't expect that reading a few paragraphs and answering some questions is going to give you the clarity and peace of mind that you're looking for. Many people struggle with these decisions for months if not years before they're ready to act. If that's the case for you, it's okay. Give yourself permission to think about your options, feel your feelings, consult with trusted advisors (like close friends or counselors), meditate, or pray. You don't need to decide right now. But come back to these questions, continue to tune in to your thoughts, feelings, and needs, and to value them—rather than avoiding or minimizing them. If you do this, you'll make the best decision for yourself in time. Also, remember that when you ask a lot of yourself (like making a difficult decision), you need to give more to yourself in the form of self-care. So, be kind to yourself and treat yourself well.

Summary

In this chapter, we discussed the importance of using consequences, not punishments, when our boundaries are crossed; if we don't, our boundaries become meaningless. However, enforcing consequences is challenging for many of the same reasons that setting boundaries is challenging. Sometimes, boundary violations don't leave us any good choices; we may ultimately realize that the only way to regain safety, self-respect, and well-being is to end a relationship, leave a job, move, or give up something else that's important to us. Although you still may find enforcing consequences challenging, I hope that you now feel more confident and prepared to implement them. Moving forward, we'll focus on boundary skills in specific contexts.

Part Three

PRACTICING BOUNDARY SKILLS WITH OTHERS

Chapter 7

Boundary Skills at Work

In part one of this workbook, you learned about what boundaries are and why they're important. And in part two, you built your boundary-setting skills. Now, in part three, you'll practice boundary skills in different areas of your life. The boundary skills you've learned so far are a strong foundation on which to build more specialized skills for setting boundaries in specific contexts. In this chapter, we'll discuss ways to handle boundary issues at work.

Why We Need Boundaries at Work

Has your boss ever given you more work than you could accomplish during your work hours? Have you ever had a coworker who slacks off, leaving you to do everything? How about a coworker who constantly interrupts or intrudes on your personal space? Certainly, we've all had a coworker who reheats fish in the microwave, seemingly oblivious to the foul smell left throughout the office. And while these are fairly minor boundary issues, they can make work unpleasant and frustrating. More extreme work-related boundary issues, such as sexual harassment, not being paid, or being expected to work without safety equipment, can have serious negative effects on our health and happiness at work and spill over into our personal lives as well.

Your boundaries at work tell your boss, coworkers, customers, and others how they can treat you or what you're willing to do. They protect you from being mistreated, taken advantage of, overworked, or physically hurt. Boundaries at work also define what you're responsible for and not responsible for. Let's take a closer look at some examples of work-related boundary issues to see how they can play out.

For the past two years, Arnav, twenty-six, has worked in the marketing department of a large retailer. He loves the fast pace and opportunities to learn from more seasoned professionals. Arnav works closely with Ian, who's been with the company for fifteen years and is highly respected. Recently, Ian has been lukewarm about all of Arnav's ideas, telling him they're "over the top" or "not going to appeal to our demographics." Arnav was disappointed because he'd worked hard on the concepts but figured that Ian was right. So, when Ian took credit for one of Arnav's ideas, he was shocked. But Ian blew off his concerns, saying, "What's the big deal? You have tons of ideas and I needed a win." So, Arnav let it go. Two months later, Ian again claimed one of Arnav's ideas as his own.

Audrey is an hourly employee at a medical clinic. She's supposed to clock out at 3:00 p.m. sharp but routinely stays late to complete required paperwork. Also, her boss frequently calls her in the evenings with questions or insists that on her days off she make lengthy calls to insurance companies to get time-sensitive treatment authorizations. Initially, Audrey put up with this because she wanted to make a good impression and all her coworkers seemed to do it. But she feels resentful and taken advantage of because her employer refuses to pay her for the extra hours she works. She thinks about quitting all the time but doesn't want to abandon her patients.

Do these stories sound familiar? Both Arnav and Audrey care about their work and want to do a good job, but they don't set boundaries to protect themselves. Arnav's productivity and confidence took a big hit when Ian betrayed him. He felt stupid and naïve for trusting Ian in the first place. And Audrey was understandably so frustrated that she was on the verge of quitting. Her time wasn't respected, and she was expected to work without getting paid. Arnav and Audrey both suffered because they didn't have adequate boundaries at work.

Think about your current work situation. (If you're not currently doing paid work, you can refer to volunteer work or a previous job.) What boundary issues have you experienced at work? How did they affect your job performance, job satisfaction, and personal life?

_____

_____

_____

_____

_____

Now that you've read Arnav's and Audrey's stories, and thought about your own work-related boundary problems, you have a good idea of why we need to set boundaries at work. Now, let's talk about what stands in our way and how we can overcome these barriers.

Overcoming Barriers to Setting Boundaries at Work

In some ways, setting boundaries at work is the same as setting boundaries in your personal life. You can use the Four Steps to Setting Better Boundaries (chapter 4) and tips for communicating your boundaries (chapter 5) to guide your process. However, work relationships, roles, norms, and power differentials can also present some particular challenges.

Many people struggle to set workplace boundaries because they have a lot to lose—most notably their jobs. They're understandably worried that if they set boundaries, they'll be fired (or punished in some other way). Of course, I can't promise you that setting boundaries at work, or anywhere else, won't have any negative or unexpected consequences. But there are also negative consequences of not setting boundaries, often more serious consequences than Arnav and Audrey experienced. So, as you read the rest of this chapter, weigh the pros and cons of setting boundaries in your work situation.

Dealing with Feelings of Powerlessness

If we're going to set boundaries, we must overcome the false belief that we don't have the right to set boundaries or be treated fairly. In chapter 3, you identified your personal rights and recognized that you, like everyone else, has certain basic rights. That list of personal rights applies to both your personal life and your workplace.

However, it can be helpful, especially if you feel powerless or uncertain of your rights in the workplace, to identify more rights specific to your job. I've tried to list rights that seem universal, but depending on your work situation or location, your rights may vary. Here are some examples of workplace rights:

- I have the right to be treated with respect.
- I have the right to not be discriminated against based on my gender, race, sexual orientation, religion, age, or disability.
- I have the right to be paid according to the terms agreed upon.
- I have the right to time off.
- I have the right to say no.
- I have the right to a safe workplace.
- I have the right to be given credit for the work I've done.
- I have the right to the equipment or materials needed to do my job safely.

- I have the right to _____.
- I have the right to _____.
- I have the right to _____.

With your rights in mind, what boundaries do you need to set at work?

_____

_____

_____

_____

_____

Recognizing that you have rights and asking that they be respected doesn't mean that they will be. Our power primarily lies in being able to meet our own needs when we can't rely on others to understand and meet them.

If the other people involved aren't willing or able to change, is there a way for you to meet your underlying needs yourself? And if not, what other options do you see?

_____

_____

_____

_____

_____

Unfortunately, another obstacle we face in setting and enforcing boundaries at work is that we may not have as many choices as we do in our personal lives.

Dealing with Limited Choices

Most of us don't have as much freedom at work as we do at home. There are more rules to follow and a hierarchy of people who make decisions for and about us. However, this doesn't mean that you're powerless or can't set boundaries. It may mean that you have fewer choices for dealing with boundary issues at work, as you'll see in Derek's story.

As a receptionist at a busy law firm, Derek is required to sit at the front desk, answer the telephone, greet clients, and do assorted administrative tasks. He's friendly with many of his coworkers, including one of the attorneys, Marina, who generously brings him a cup of his favorite coffee every morning. But when Marina delivers the coffee, she pulls up a chair and vents about her problems for twenty minutes. Although Derek likes Marina and appreciates that she brings him coffee, he's busy and finds her negativity draining. Repeatedly, he's explained to Marina that he doesn't have time to chat with her, but she persists. Derek feels stuck. His job makes it impossible for him to avoid Marina.

The fact that Derek works with Marina means he must see her five days per week. If a stranger kept talking to him while he worked at the library or coffee shop, he could get up and move, but he can't move his desk or change his work hours. Derek has limited choices for how to address Marina's boundary violation, but he still has options. For example, he could schedule a more convenient time to chat with Marina (such as over lunch), continue to kindly and directly tell her that he's not available to talk, ask his supervisor to speak to Marina, or change their routine by giving up coffee for a couple of weeks or taking a few days off.

None of these choices may be ideal, but they're probably better than Derek quitting a job that he likes and is good at or suffering endlessly because he feels hopeless and powerless to change his situation. The point is that it's much easier to notice what we can't do and think of reasons we can't solve our boundary problems than it is to accept imperfect solutions.

When you identify options for handling boundary problems at work, notice whether you feel any resistance or judgment about them. For example, you might think, *That's a dumb idea* or *I don't want to be a snitch*. Use the following chart to explore your feelings. Be curious about what this resistance or judgment means and see whether you can find a more positive way to look at your options.

Options for Addressing Boundary Problems	Resistance or Judgment	Potential Positive Outcome
Example: Ask my supervisor to talk to Marina	Afraid my supervisor will be annoyed and think less of me	My supervisor will be supportive because I'm a good employee and I want to get my work done

In addition, the amount of power you have at your workplace will influence how you set boundaries.

Dealing with Power Differentials

Sometimes difficulty with setting boundaries at work is related to being in a subordinate role or not having as much authority as others. The reality is that, despite our self-advocacy skills and willingness to change what's in our control, we can't always solve our work-related boundary problems alone. You may not have the power you need to physically distance yourself from an abusive coworker or the resources to get your employer to pay you for the overtime you worked. In this case, you may need to ask someone who has more power and resources, such as the human resources director, labor board, an attorney, your union representative, law enforcement, or someone higher up at the company, to intervene and enforce your rights. You may need to seek outside help in these situations:

- You've tried to resolve the issue yourself and things haven't improved.

- Your direct supervisor has dismissed your concerns, refused to investigate, or instructed you not to report the problem.

- You're afraid for your safety or the safety of others.

- You're being physically abused, harassed, or denigrated.

- You're being discriminated against based on your gender, race, religion, sexual orientation, age, or ability.

- Your physical or mental health is suffering because of your work situation.

- Your employer, colleague, or supervisor has asked or forced you to do something dangerous, illegal, or unethical.

- You've been threatened (with harm, being fired or demoted, a less desirable schedule, etc.) if you report dangerous, illegal, or unethical behavior.

- Your employer is breaking the law (for example, you're not being paid for the hours you worked or given required breaks).

- Other: _____

- Other: _____

Unlike a personal relationship, your employer may be less interested in how you feel about the way you've been treated at work and more interested in protecting their own interests. So, if you decide to seek help from your superior or someone outside of the company, be prepared with details about what's happened (dates, witnesses, exactly what was said or done), and what you want them to do about it.

It can be anxiety-producing to seek help with work-related boundary issues—even when you know that your rights are being trampled and it's unlikely that you can resolve the issues yourself. I often find that people would rather quit their jobs than seek help. When you quit, there's an illusion of being in control, whereas seeking help (and potentially getting fired, embarrassed, or labeled a troublemaker) can feel powerless. But quitting is rarely the outcome people really want. So, sort through your feelings and options to figure out the best course of action.

Have you ever felt like the only way to solve your boundary issues at work is to quit? If you're ever in this situation, notice what feelings come up when you think about seeking help. What feels difficult, stressful, or scary about it?

_____

_____

_____

_____

_____

What is the outcome you ultimately want? How likely are you to achieve this outcome yourself?

_____

_____

_____

_____

_____

There's no guarantee, of course, that seeking help will get you the result that you want. You'll need to weigh the potential benefits against the potential drawbacks. And when it comes to your job, paycheck, and professional standing, you need to consider your options carefully.

What do you see as the potential benefits and risks of seeking help? How likely are you to achieve your desired outcome with help?

_____

_____

_____

_____

_____

I wish I could tell you that setting boundaries at work (or in any situation) will always turn out in your favor, but that would be naïve. Unfortunately, some people and institutions resist treating others with respect and will take advantage of people for as long as they can. So, it's possible that in extreme situations, leaving your job may be the only way to protect yourself from mistreatment. Even so, think about what you might gain by setting boundaries at work.

What might you gain by setting boundaries at work even if they aren't entirely successful? What would attempting to set boundaries and be assertive at work say about you? Alternatively, what would being passive at work tell your colleagues and employer?

_____

_____

_____

_____

_____

I hope you find that standing up for yourself is a worthy endeavor, a reflection of your right to respectful and fair treatment, and a step toward being more confident and assertive, even if others are unwilling to listen. You can also find a list of employment rights resources in the Resources page at http://www.newharbinger.com/47582.

Summary

Setting boundaries at work requires many of the same skills that we use in our personal lives, but it can be extra challenging because our jobs are at stake and we may not have the power to change our environments, schedules, or the people we interact with. This chapter reviewed your personal rights at work, addressed power differentials, and explored when and whether to seek outside help with work-related boundary problems. In chapter 8, you'll learn about setting boundaries with your partner.

Chapter 8

Boundary Skills with Your Partner

Often, romantic relationships are our most challenging relationships. And many of these difficulties are the result of boundary problems—not having clear agreements about what you're each responsible for and what kind of behavior is acceptable in your relationship. In this chapter, you'll learn the skills you need to resolve boundary issues with your partner and create a more fulfilling, less conflicted relationship.

Boundaries Build Strong Connections

Are you concerned that boundaries will create distance or conflict between you and your partner? If so, you're not alone, and it makes sense that you're nervous about setting boundaries.

But think about what happens when you don't have boundaries. Without boundaries, you might feel smothered or controlled by your partner, like you've lost your identity or independence. Or your relationship might be fraught with conflicts, disappointments, and hurt feelings because you don't have clear agreements about how to behave or who's responsible for shared work.

Fortunately, healthy boundaries can help you create just the right amount of connection and separateness in your relationship, so you have the trust and intimacy that you desire while also maintaining your individuality. Boundaries also reduce conflict, blame, and resentment because they delineate who's responsible for what in a partnership, and they protect your relationship from outside threats, such as infidelity, time-consuming hobbies, or prioritizing your parents or friends over your partner.

How have boundary issues contributed to problems with your current or past partner(s)?

_____

_____

_____

_____

_____

How do you hope boundaries will improve your relationship with your partner (or future partner)?

_____

_____

_____

_____

_____

Let's take a closer look at some of the most common boundary issues that partners have, so we can understand and resolve them.

Common Boundary Issues

Keith and Cassandra both have an ongoing boundary issue with their partners. As you read their stories, notice how their partners violate their boundaries, how their needs go unmet, and how it negatively impacts their relationships.

Keith is a private person. He doesn't have many close friends and he rarely shares his problems or feelings with the friends he does have. His girlfriend, Cheryl, is the opposite; she's outgoing and thrives on deep friendships. So, when she and Keith started having relationship problems, she didn't think twice about telling her friends that Keith was depressed and taking medication. When Keith found out that Cheryl had shared these personal details, he felt betrayed. He was embarrassed and angry that Cheryl had crossed this line.

Cassandra and Lena had been arguing about their finances since they got married two years ago. Cassandra wanted to save for a house and so she could take time off from work when they have children. Lena said she wanted the same things, but she continued to make large purchases without consulting Cassandra, which added to their credit card debt. They tried to make a budget together, but Lena didn't stick to it, and continued to buy things Cassandra thought were unnecessary. Cassandra saw her financial goals slipping away and felt Lena's actions were disrespectful and unloving.

Can you relate to Keith or Cassandra or their partners? Most of us have been on both sides of boundary issues with our partner—we've had our boundaries violated and we've violated our partner's boundaries.

Boundaries are the agreements that govern our relationships and some, like an agreement to spend quality time together on Saturday nights, support healthy relationships; other agreements, such as agreeing to call each other derogatory names, don't. Now, it's unlikely that anyone would make a formal agreement to call each other names. Instead, these agreements develop over time because either no one objected to the name-calling or there weren't meaningful consequences for doing it. Essentially, if a behavior is tolerated, it becomes acceptable by default.

The most common problems in a marriage or partnership—issues of fidelity, communication, privacy, how money and time are spent, divvying up household responsibilities, and when and how often to be sexually intimate—are all boundary problems at their core. As we look at each of these issues, try to identify the spoken and unspoken agreements you have with your partner about these issues.

Fidelity

Fidelity in an intimate relationship usually refers to remaining sexually faithful to your partner. However, these days most people recognize that emotional infidelity is both common and painful and therefore worth including in agreements about fidelity. Fidelity boundaries define whether you can be sexually or emotionally intimate with someone other than your primary partner and if so, with whom, when, where, and in what ways.

Communication

Communication boundaries refer to the way you and your partner want to share information. They include when and how you discuss important issues, how you argue, whether you take time-outs from difficult conversations, whether it's okay to call each other names, what you talk about in person versus by text or phone, and so forth.

Privacy

Privacy boundaries are agreements about what should be shared with your partner and what's okay to share with people outside your relationship. An important privacy boundary is how you differentiate privacy and secrecy.

Money

Money boundaries are agreements about how you use shared assets and make financial decisions. They include setting financial goals, decisions about purchases, and whether you consult each other before making purchases.

Time

Time boundaries refer to how much time you spend with your partner, what you do together, how much and when you will have personal time, and when you will be at home.

Household Responsibilities

Household boundaries are agreements about who is responsible for the tasks required to run your household and when these tasks will be completed, including childcare, cooking, paying bills, filing taxes, mowing the lawn, purchasing gifts, and so forth.

Parenting

These are agreements about how you'll parent your children, including how you make decisions about their health and education, discipline them and set rules, and what information you share with your children.

Sex

Sexual boundaries refer to what sexual activities you'll engage in, when, where, and how often. They can include agreements about initiating sex, changing your mind once sexual activity has begun, practicing safer sex, getting tested for sexually transmitted diseases, or viewing pornography.

Think about the agreements you have with your partner. Which agreements work well?

_____

_____

_____

_____

_____

Which areas cause conflict because one or both of you violate the agreements (or perhaps no agreements were ever made)?

_____

_____

_____

_____

_____

If your relationship has numerous conflicts or boundary issues, you may be eager to change them all. This is understandable, but may be overwhelming for you and your partner, so it's best to start with just one boundary issue. Use the space that follows to identify the issue you most want to work on and describe the agreement that you'd like to have with your partner about this issue. This isn't a list of demands, so try to write your desired agreement using the words "us" or "we."

Cassandra's example: We'll automatically transfer $500 into our savings account monthly to save for the future. We'll use a weekly cash allowance for all our purchases except groceries and gas.

_____

_____

_____

_____

_____

What you just wrote is an agreement that meets *your* needs. And while it's important to know what you need, your partner may have different needs. In a partnership, it's important to consider everyone's needs, not just your own. So, what can you do if your needs conflict with your partner's?

Conflicting Needs

Boundary issues also occur when your needs, values, or priorities conflict with your partner's. As you read Nina's story, think about what she needs and values and how that compares to her husband's needs and values.

Nina and Arthur have been married for thirty-five years and have had a long-standing conflict over the amount of time he spends golfing. Over the years, Nina has asked Arthur to spend more quality time with her. She's booked weekend getaways for them and tried to find hobbies they both enjoy. But Arthur loves golfing and isn't willing to cut back. Nina thinks Arthur prefers golf and his buddies over her and feels rejected and hurt. Arthur considers golfing time well spent; he gets to exercise, spend time outside, and socialize all at the same time. From his perspective, he spends plenty of time with his wife.

As you can see, Nina needs more connection and quality time with Arthur and feels dissatisfied because she's not getting it. In contrast, Arthur doesn't need as much quality time with his wife to feel happy and connected. His other needs are getting met by playing golf. It's important to note that Nina's needs aren't more important than Arthur's and he's not a bad person because he doesn't need or want to spend more time with his wife. The problem is that they can't find a solution that meets both of their needs.

It's normal to have differing needs, so we can't completely eliminate these kinds of boundary issues. It's unrealistic, of course, to expect that you'll always want to have sex when your partner does or that you'll both need the same amount of time alone. And yet, many of us routinely deny our needs, wants, goals, or values to please our partner and avoid conflicts. We take what psychotherapist Terence Real calls the "one-down" position based on feelings of inferiority. In *The New Rules of Marriage*, Real (2008) cautions that "if you don't stand up for your needs, you begin shutting them down, often feeling like a resentful victim" (124). In other words, talking to your partner about your needs is best for everyone; denying your needs will infect your relationship with bitterness and discontent. And it's your ability to resolve, not avoid, boundary conflicts that will help create a satisfying relationship.

Resolving Boundary Issues with Your Partner

To resolve your boundary issues, you and your partner both have to directly ask for what you need, be interested in each other's needs and feelings, compromise when appropriate, and accept that sometimes your partner won't be able to meet your needs.

Be Direct

Your partner can't read your mind. You've heard this a hundred times, but don't you sometimes expect (or at least wish) that your partner will know what you need and give it to you without having to ask? Certainly, life would be easier if this were true, but it's unrealistic and, therefore, unhelpful.

To create healthy relationship boundaries or agreements, you must directly and respectfully ask for what you need and be open to reasonable compromises. Using the I-statement formula from chapter 5 will help you be assertive, not aggressive or accusatory, and this will make it easier for your partner to understand your feelings and needs.

Be Interested in Your Partner's Needs and Feelings

Relationships are reciprocal. So, if yours is going to work, you have to communicate your needs, wants, and feelings *and* you have to be interested in your partner's needs, wants, and feelings.

This is challenging when your needs aren't getting met or there's a high level of conflict in your relationship, but it is possible! If you're feeling disconnected from or disinterested in your partner's needs, try using some of the phrases below to begin investigating and understanding their needs. These statements may feel contrived, but they can gradually build positive feelings and open communication. Here are some examples:

- What do you need (or want)?

- I need (or want) _____. Does that work for you?

- We seem to be out of sync. I'd like to understand what you want or need so we can figure out how to compromise.

- I care about you and your feelings.

Also, try to notice observable signs that your partner is in distress, such as crying, yelling, shaking, pacing, staying in bed, drinking, or isolating. However, it's *not* your job to intuit what they need entirely on your own. In most situations, it's okay to ask what they need, but ultimately, it's their job to directly and respectfully communicate their needs.

Asking what someone needs doesn't commit you to meeting the need. But when you ask with empathy, it communicates that you care and sets you up to find a solution that satisfies both of your needs to the best of your ability.

Be Open to Compromise

Most boundary conflicts can be resolved through compromise if you're both willing to give a bit. Even though we talked about compromise in chapter 5, it's worth a more in-depth discussion here.

Compromise can happen in a few ways. Let's say you came home late from a long day at work, and you're exhausted and need sleep. But your partner's primary need is to connect and spend time with you. You both can't get all of what you need at the same time. But when you compromise, you both get some of what you need. That could mean you spend thirty minutes together (instead of sixty) and then you go to bed. Or you could go to bed immediately because you're extremely tired and agree to spend time connecting with your partner the next morning.

When you negotiate, consider whether a need is time-sensitive, how strong the need is, and whether someone will be harmed if the need is delayed or not met completely. You can even say, "My need for sleep is a 10 right now. How strong is your need to connect?" If you can both honestly assess the intensity of your needs, this can be a simple and effective tool to help you compromise. Let's use Diana's story to think about different ways couples can compromise and still have their needs met.

Six years ago, Diana's husband had an affair with a woman he met on a business trip. Since then, they've attended therapy and their relationship has improved significantly. However, Diana objects to her husband "following" female models and sexualized fitness gurus on social media, commenting on their posts, and sending them private messages. Her husband insists it's all innocent and wants Diana to stop checking up on him.

When we consider how Diana and her husband can compromise, we're essentially asking, *How can they both get what they need?* So, we first want to identify their needs using the list of Universal Human Needs in the Appendix.

What does Diana need?

_____

_____

What does her husband need?

_____

_____

What are some ways for Diana and her husband to get their needs met sufficiently for both to feel satisfied?

_____

_____

_____

_____

_____

Compromising on an issue such as this is often hard because we have strong feelings about fidelity, especially when there's been a betrayal, as there was for Diana. And when we feel strongly or place a high value on something, it's harder to be flexible and open to compromise. For example, if you feel strongly about how your children are disciplined and your partner either agrees with your approach or doesn't feel strongly about this issue, you'll have few conflicts and they'll be easily resolved. But if you and your partner believe strongly in different approaches to discipline, compromise will be more difficult.

What boundary issues with your partner do you feel strongly about or place a high value on?

_____

_____

_____

_____

What issues do you think your partner feels strongly about or places a high value on?

_____

_____

_____

_____

Being aware of your and your partner's "hot button" issues can help you approach compromise with more empathy and openness to change. If you're having trouble compromising, the following questions can help you.

Why do I feel so strongly about this? Is there a way for me to flex a little without giving up an important value or need?

_____

_____

_____

_____

Even when both partners feel strongly about something, most boundary issues can be resolved through compromise when you're committed to each other and to working together to resolve your differences. However, we all have some nonnegotiable boundaries that help keep us safe. So, there will be a few issues that you and your partner are each unwilling to compromise on. Still, these should be few and far between.

If there's an issue that you can't compromise on, you'll need to consider whether you can accept things as they are. Here are some questions that can help you determine your next steps if you reach an impasse:

- Can you accept that this is a nonnegotiable boundary for your partner?

- Is this a need that you can meet yourself?

- What is the "cost" of accepting things as they are?

- How often is your partner unwilling or unable to compromise?

Compromise is a skill that most people can learn. It requires empathy and the ability to go without or delay gratification. If you or your partner struggle with empathy or impulsivity, compromise may be more difficult. This doesn't mean it's impossible, but I encourage you to ask your partner and yourself whether you're willing to practice and get some help from a relationship therapist, if needed.

See a Relationship Therapist

If you've been practicing the skills in this book and things aren't improving (or they're getting worse) or your relationship has been highly conflicted or unfulfilling for more than a couple of months, it's probably time to get help from a relationship therapist. A skilled therapist can help you heal wounds and learn new skills in a safe environment.

It's normal to be ambivalent about therapy. It's hard work, very emotional, and the stakes are high when your relationship is on the line. It's tempting to avoid dealing with relationship problems, too. But time alone rarely resolves them. So, if you think therapy might improve your relationship, talk to your partner about it. Use the assertive communication skills you've been learning, share your feelings, and explain why you'd like your partner to participate. Here's an example.

I've been feeling frustrated and sad about our relationship problems for quite a while. It doesn't seem like things are getting better. So, I'd like us to get couples counseling. I think talking to a professional who's neutral about this would help us both. It would mean a lot to me if you would come.

If your partner refuses, consider going without them. You can still learn a lot and get the support you need.

Summary

In this chapter, we focused on understanding how boundaries can improve your relationship with your partner and we explored common boundary issues you may face. You also honed your communication skills, including assertiveness, staying interested and invested in your partner's needs, and compromising, which will help you resolve boundary conflicts. In chapter 9, we'll continue to build boundary skills, but pivot to setting boundaries with our children.

Chapter 9

Boundary Skills with Your Children

If you're a parent, do you ever feel like all you do is say no? Whether you're parenting toddlers or teenagers, setting limits, saying no, and doling out consequences is exhausting! Children are naturally curious, they push for independence (usually before they're ready), and they test limits. So, setting boundaries with them is relentless. And that's why we'll spend this chapter discussing the importance of persevering in setting boundaries with our children and how to do it more effectively, so we don't get so discouraged and frustrated.

Why Children Need Boundaries

As you know from your own experience, or from reading this book, witnessing and learning about healthy boundaries as a child helps us establish well-functioning boundaries in adulthood. When we set boundaries with our children, we're teaching them about responsibility, assertiveness, self-management, and other skills they will need to be physically and emotionally healthy and successful. But before we delve into why children need boundaries, let's look at what happens when parents don't set appropriate boundaries with their children.

Orlando has always been a strong-willed child. As a toddler, he would cry and throw tantrums for hours when he didn't get his way. His parents were constantly overwhelmed and embarrassed by Orlando's behavior, so they started giving in to his demands and buying him candy and toys to keep him quiet while they shopped. Now, at age nine, he stays up until midnight, eats whatever he wants, and spends hours in front of a screen. Occasionally his parents threaten to take away his computer, but they never follow through. Orlando is tired and moody, bullies kids at school, has few friends because he's bossy and selfish, and doesn't do his homework.

When Alyssa's father suddenly left three years ago, it was devastating emotionally and financially for Alyssa and her mother. Alyssa, now fifteen, became her mother's confidante, providing her mother emotional support as she tried to put her life back together. Alyssa loves that she's her mother's best friend, but she feels uncomfortable when her mother talks about her sex life or bad-mouths her father, and sometimes she wishes she could hang out with her friends more. Alyssa doesn't know how to tell her mother how she feels or what she wants. She knows her mom's been through a lot and doesn't want to cause her any more pain.

These stories show us two very different outcomes caused by the lack of appropriate parental boundaries. Orlando is self-centered and noncompliant, while Alyssa is selfless and overly compliant. We can imagine how these problems will be magnified as Orlando and Alyssa grow up. Orlando likely will become an adult who doesn't respect other people's boundaries, feels entitled, and takes advantage of others. He isn't developing self-discipline or frustration tolerance because he never has to wait or accept limits, so he'll anger easily and struggle to manage his drinking, eating, spending, and time. Alyssa's enmeshed relationship with her mother will probably become the blueprint for her future relationships with friends and lovers. She may continue to feel responsible for other people's needs and feelings while suppressing her own and not feeling confident or safe enough to ask for what she needs and wants.

Neither outcome is what we want for our children now or in the future. So, in the rest of this chapter, we'll discuss how boundaries can help us raise children who respect themselves and others.

Boundaries Keep Children Safe

First and foremost, boundaries are limits or rules that keep children physically and emotionally safe. Safety is a primary need; without it, children have a hard time developing emotionally and cognitively, expressing their feelings and ideas, forming positive relationships, learning, and setting long-term goals.

Let's think about babies and toddlers for a moment. They need parents to tell or show them what's safe and what isn't. Otherwise, they might run into the street or touch a hot pan. As children grow, they learn more about what's dangerous. They may get burned, for example, and learn not to touch a hot pan.

But it's not just babies and toddlers who need boundaries; even older teens need rules and limits to keep them safe. The prefrontal cortex, the part of the brain that is capable of abstract thinking and allows us to predict the consequences of our actions, isn't fully developed until late adolescence or early adulthood. We all know teenagers who drive too fast, use drugs or alcohol, have unprotected sex, or do other risky things (you may have even been one yourself). And while parents can't control everything their teenagers do, rules and consequences guide teenagers toward better decisions that will reduce their risks and set them up for success in adulthood.

Boundaries Teach Children to Be Responsible

One of our goals as parents is to raise children who will become self-sufficient adults. We want them to be able to take care of themselves and not rely on us to meet their needs indefinitely. For this to happen, we need to teach them what they're responsible for. For example, my twelve-year-old often asks me to make his lunch. I could easily do it for him, but I want him to take responsibility for things he's capable of doing. So, I choose to say no, and let him make his own lunch.

Boundaries also teach children what they aren't responsible for. Children get confused about their responsibilities when there aren't boundaries to differentiate roles and responsibilities. Consider Alyssa. Her mother treated her as a peer and had inappropriate conversations with her, which made Alyssa feel responsible for her mother's happiness. Children shouldn't be responsible for meeting their parents' emotional needs—being their friend, giving them advice, or making them happy—and boundaries show children that they aren't responsible for these things.

Having clear boundaries teaches children that they are responsible for their behavior and that their actions have consequences. Boundaries also encourage children to plan ahead and manage their behavior. For example, if my son doesn't make his lunch, he'll be hungry, or if he talks back in class, he'll get detention. Anticipating consequences and learning self-management teaches children to make safe and healthy choices for themselves, rather than just doing what feels good in the moment.

Boundaries Teach Children How to Be Assertive

When you set boundaries with your children, you're showing them how to be assertive. In chapter 5, you read about the importance of assertive communication, how standing up for yourself protects you from being mistreated or taken advantage of, helps you solve problems, and allows you to communicate your needs without being mean or hurtful. As your children get older, they'll spend more and more time out in the world without you there to speak for them or protect them. So, we need to encourage children to value their own needs and to say "no" or "stop" when someone is doing something unsafe, hurtful, or uncomfortable.

Boundaries Teach Children to Respect Others

Boundaries teach children to accept limits, that the world doesn't revolve around them, that sometimes the answer is "no," and that they need to compromise and consider other people's needs, opinions, and beliefs. Boundaries encourage children to think beyond themselves and try to understand what other people feel or need, which helps them develop compassion and empathy for others.

Reflecting on what you read about how children can benefit from boundaries, what do you hope your children will learn or gain when you set boundaries with them?

_____

_____

_____

_____

_____

Now that we've established how important boundaries are for children in general, and you've identified how your children can benefit from better boundaries, let's do some troubleshooting.

Tips for Setting Boundaries with Your Children

Setting boundaries with your children is hard work, and there are numerous ways we can get tripped up. Having been a psychotherapist for twenty-five years and a parent for nearly twenty years, I've repeatedly witnessed parents making several boundary-setting errors:

- They have unrealistic expectations given their child's age or developmental level.

- They don't enforce boundaries consistently.

- They have too many rules and illogical consequences.

- They lose their cool and overreact.

In this section, we'll focus on how to adjust in these areas.

Some of you will see significant improvements by making the modest changes suggested in this chapter. However, if you continue to struggle with your child, I recommend getting guidance and support from a professional, such as your child's pediatrician or a child therapist or psychologist. This can be the best thing you do for yourself and your child, because even though setting boundaries is hard, it shouldn't routinely cause you sleepless nights, stress-related health problems, fear, or uncontrollable anger. For more information, a list of recommended parenting books is available in the Resources page at http://www.newharbinger.com/47582.

Boundaries Need to Be Developmentally Appropriate

The boundaries that you set for your children need to change as they mature. You obviously wouldn't have the same expectations and rules for a two-year-old and a fourteen-year-old because they have different needs and abilities. As children grow, they're physically able to do more for themselves, they gradually learn to control their emotions and behaviors, and their thinking expands from concrete (what they can observe) to abstract (being able to imagine things they've never experienced, make predictions or inferences, plan, and so forth).

Parents often overestimate what their children can cognitively and emotionally understand, and as a result they set unrealistic expectations and rules. For example, if I tell a two-year-old not to eat the cookies I put in front of her, and then give her a time-out when she does, I've set an unrealistic expectation because two-year-olds don't have this much self-control. And I've unfairly punished her for violating a boundary that wasn't realistic for her developmental level.

Since it's important to keep our children's developmental level in mind, the following is an overview of typical cognitive and social-emotional development in children. However, your child may develop at a different pace and have strengths and weaknesses—such as good organizational skills or difficulty reading facial expressions—that differ from his peers, which you should consider when setting boundaries.

Age 0–1: During their first year, children bond with their caregivers, learn to smile and interact with others, and begin to say simple words and explore their environments. When parents are consistently attentive and meet their child's needs, trust and a secure attachment develop; the child learns that her needs will be met, and that the world is safe. At about seven months, babies recognize themselves as separate from their parents, which can cause distress when they're left alone. By twelve months, most babies are crawling or beginning to walk. Your focus should be on creating a secure attachment with your child by being attentive to his needs. Any boundaries that you set should relate to keeping your child safe.

Age 1–2: During their second year, children want greater independence. They learn that they can do things to get a response from you. For example, babies love to throw their spoon on the floor and watch you pick it up repeatedly. This is tiresome for adults but fascinating for little ones who are just learning about cause and effect. Your child isn't intentionally trying to annoy you because he isn't able to consider your perspective yet. Children at this stage learn by doing and touching, which is why it's important to give them the freedom to safely explore and experiment while continuing to provide consistency and safe limits.

Age 2–5: At about two years old, children learn the power of no. They adamantly exert their independence by saying no and testing limits. They experience more complex emotions but don't know appropriate ways to express their feelings or solve problems (hence, the tantrums that are common during this stage). They begin to understand simple rules and consequences, although they remain self-centered, unable to see other people's perspectives, and have limited self-control and patience. Naming their feelings and redirecting them to appropriate activities are helpful strategies for parenting children this age.

Age 5–11: As children begin school, they improve at following basic rules. They're better able to consider other people's feelings and needs, share, and take turns, and friends become more important. According to psychologist Jean Piaget's theory of cognitive development, logical reasoning develops between ages seven and eleven, and children in this age range can consider multiple aspects of a problem or situation and remember and follow multistep instructions. However, their thinking is still mostly concrete and focused on the present. During this stage, children can be responsible for simple chores, like brushing their teeth or clearing the table, and they can earn privileges by doing chores. However, they continue to need reminders, accountability (like a chore chart), or rewards to complete unpleasant tasks.

Age 12–18: During adolescence, children work on developing their own identity and gaining independence from their parents. They explore their values, beliefs, and interests and make more independent decisions. Their abstract thinking develops, which means teens can solve more complex problems, understand cause and effect, and better plan and organize. However, this is a slow process and frequently teens don't accurately think through the consequences of their actions. They're also highly influenced by their peers and have a strong need for acceptance, which can lead to risky behavior. Changing hormone levels during puberty contribute to mood swings, and it's normal for adolescents to still struggle to understand and regulate strong feelings. In terms of boundaries, our goal isn't to control but to guide our teenagers toward taking responsibility for their decisions. Parents need to balance limits with giving their teenagers the freedom to make mistakes and learn from them.

Given what you just read, what do you think your child is developmentally able to do or not do?

_____

_____

_____

_____

_____

With your child's developmental stage in mind, do you think any of your rules or expectations are unrealistic? If so, which ones? How might you make them more developmentally appropriate?

_____

_____

_____

_____

_____

Do you have any questions about your child's development or abilities? Note those that you'd like to research further or discuss with a professional.

_____

_____

_____

_____

_____

Be Consistent

Children of all ages need clear and consistent boundaries and need to know what will happen if they don't respect them. Imagine starting a new job and not being given any directions; you don't know what to do or when to do it. Sometimes you're praised for showing up at 9 a.m., sometimes you're ignored, and sometimes you're reprimanded. This sounds confusing and frustrating, right? This is what it's like for our children when we change the rules without warning or selectively enforce rules based on our moods or energy level.

At the same time, we shouldn't expect perfection from ourselves. We're all inconsistent at times, but we can strive to communicate clearly and stay true to our word more often than not. Let's start by assessing your consistency with boundaries. Then you'll identify steps you can take to be more consistent.

What gets in the way of you being consistent? Use a scale of 1 to 10 to rate each option.

_____ Being tired or overwhelmed

_____ Disagreeing with my partner or children's other parent about rules and consequences

_____ Anger

_____ Guilt

_____ Fear

_____ Wanting my child to like me

_____ Not knowing what appropriate boundaries and consequences are

_____ Other: _____

For the items you rated as a 5 or higher, what would help you address these barriers? For example, if anger is a barrier for you, would you benefit from taking an anger management class, getting more sleep, or meditating? If you feel stuck, try to identify *why* you're experiencing these obstacles.

_____

_____

_____

_____

_____

_____

_____

What specific actions can you take to overcome these obstacles and be more consistent? For instance, if you think an anger management class would be helpful, you might research classes, choose one, sign up, attend the class, and practice the skills.

1. _____

_____

2. _____

_____

3. _____

_____

4. _____

_____

5. _____

_____

Often, the barriers to consistency are complex, and you may not be able to overcome them immediately. But outlining a plan of action and taking even small steps can build positive momentum and feel hopeful.

Keep It Simple

Boundaries for children need to be easy to understand. It's tempting to make a rule for every possible situation, but this tends to be confusing for children and impossible for parents to enforce. Too many rules can also lead to power struggles in which you spend too much time and energy enforcing boundaries that aren't all that important. Power struggles can damage your relationship with your children and leave everyone frustrated and exhausted.

The most important boundaries for children of all ages are the ones that keep them physically and emotionally safe. For young children, this might be *no climbing on the bookcase*, as opposed to *you must eat three bites of broccoli*. To keep things simple, focus on boundaries that reflect your values, or what's most important to you, whether that's your children's education, manners, character, or health.

If you have a partner, I encourage you to collaborate on identifying and prioritizing boundaries for your children.

What safety-related boundaries will you prioritize with your children? Try to keep this list to three to six boundaries (fewer for younger kids, more for teenagers).

_____

_____

_____

_____

_____

What values-based boundaries will you prioritize with your children? Try to keep this list to two or three boundaries.

_____

_____

_____

_____

_____

Also, remember that strategically choosing to accept some minor boundary violations (things *not* on the lists you just made) isn't the same as being inconsistent—it's prioritizing.

Use Logical Consequences

Logical consequences are 1) directly related to the rule that was broken and 2) aim to teach children how to improve their behavior rather than shaming them or making them suffer. Logical consequences tend to be effective because they make sense to children. For example, if your child throws a toy at her sister, a logical consequence is to take away the toy. Sometimes the misbehavior creates its own logical consequence; if the toy breaks, she can't play with it—and all you have to do is let her experience the consequences of her actions. In contrast, taking away dessert is a less effective consequence because it's not related to throwing a toy.

To help you put logical consequences into practice, identify some common boundary issues for your children and some logical consequences, making sure they meet the two criteria listed above.

Boundary Issue	Logical Consequence
Example: Your son yells at you when you tell him to turn off his video game.	He isn't allowed to play video games tomorrow.

Keep Your Cool

Sometimes, strong emotions get in the way of setting boundaries. You may overreact and make unnecessarily restrictive rules and consequences (like threatening to take away your child's phone forever). Or you might be so overwhelmed and frustrated that you give up and don't enforce boundaries at all. Although I think all parents (including me) have found themselves doing these things, they're counterproductive. As parents, we need to try to stay calm, compassionate, engaged, and levelheaded, and we should strive to model effective communication skills (see chapter 5).

Most families have some recurring "boundary battles" or frequent conflicts over issues such as going to bed, eating breakfast, or coming home by curfew. Anticipating stressful situations is one way we can head off stress before it leads to out-of-control reactions.

What are your boundary battles, when do they happen, and who's involved?

_____

_____

_____

_____

_____

Eliminating boundary battles will take time and experimentation, but to get started, identify a few things you can do to make a specific situation more manageable for you and your children. This might include changing the timing, who's involved, how expectations are communicated, and so forth. For example, you might start the bedtime routine earlier, before your toddler is so tired. You may also want to ask your school-aged children for their input on how to make complying with these boundaries less stressful.

What can you do to decrease stress in boundary-setting situations?

_____

_____

_____

_____

_____

Another way to be proactive about managing stress is to include regular self-care in your routine. Which of these self-care activities help you feel good?

- Exercising

- Eating regularly and reasonably healthfully

- Getting enough sleep

- Socializing and having fun

- Sex

- Relaxation or downtime

- Medical care such as doctor's appointments

- Creative activities

- Identifying, accepting, and processing your feelings

- Time alone

- Other ideas: _____

- _____

- _____

Choose two self-care activities to prioritize. When and how will you make them more of a priority? Example: I'll take a walk at lunchtime.

_____

_____

Remember, self-care isn't all-or-nothing; every little bit helps, so don't create more stress by trying to do it all at once. Do what you can reasonably do and try to add just a little bit more self-care over the coming weeks.

In addition to preventive stress management, we also need strategies to calm and center ourselves in moments of great stress.

Review the self-soothing strategies in chapter 5 and jot down some ideas that you can use when your children are testing your patience.

_____

_____

_____

_____

_____

Managing stress is an ongoing process and can sometimes feel like a lot of work. However, even taking just a little more time for yourself and having some calming strategies ready can help you be less reactive and respond more thoughtfully and constructively to your children.

Summary

You're on your way to setting better boundaries with your children! I know you'll persevere because you know how important boundaries are for them today, and for their future success and well-being. Do your best to set boundaries that are developmentally appropriate, consistent, simple, and logical. Ask for help when you're stuck or frustrated. And be kind to yourself when you make a mistake; it's part of the process of setting boundaries with your children. Up next, you'll learn skills for setting boundaries with your extended family members and friends.

Chapter 10

Boundary Skills with Your Extended Family and Friends

Relationships with extended family members and friends enrich our lives in numerous ways. Friends and family provide emotional and practical support, opportunities for fun, and meaningful ties to our past. Still, these relationships can be fraught with tension and conflict, painful misunderstandings, and broken promises. In this chapter, we'll examine common boundary issues with family and friends and identify strategies for resolving them.

Common Boundary Issues with Family and Friends

Relationships with extended family members and friends come with expectations about how you'll interact, including how much time you spend together, how you celebrate holidays and special occasions, how you parent, handle money, and maintain privacy. In this section, we'll review common boundary issues that occur because of these expectations, and then you'll reflect on your boundary struggles in these areas.

Time Together

How much time do you want to spend interacting (in person or virtually) with your extended family and friends? Do they have the same expectations? These are the fundamental questions we need to answer when setting boundaries about time together. If we don't, we end up with problems like Anthony's and Nisha's.

Anthony's parents want to spend every holiday with him, which was fine when he was single. But now, they lay on a guilt trip when he spends alternate holidays with his boyfriend's family.

Nisha feels hurt that her best friend doesn't make any effort to call or make plans with her.

Creating boundaries about how much time you spend with your family and friends can be tricky. As our lives change—we get married, have children, move, change jobs, or have health problems—our old "agreements" about time with family and friends may no longer work. You may find yourself in a situation, like Anthony, that no longer meets your needs. Or maybe there was always a significant gap between your needs and theirs, as is the case with Nisha. Perhaps her friend doesn't feel the desire to spend as much time together as she does.

Conflicts about time spent together often come up around the holidays and other celebrations because we usually have increased expectations for family togetherness at these times.

Holidays and Special Occasions

Over my years as a psychotherapist, people have repeatedly told me that the most hurtful and egregious boundary conflicts they've experienced with extended family involved holidays and special occasions. So, if this has been your experience, you're not alone!

Holidays and special occasions, such as weddings, funerals, and births, are highly emotional, sometimes once-in-a-lifetime events, which make them ripe for boundary conflicts. We tend to have high—potentially unrealistic—expectations for these events. For example, you may dream of the perfect wedding or expect that everyone will get along at Grandma's birthday party. And when we have rigid ideas about how we want things done or what the experience should be, we're more likely to have conflicts with family or friends who have a different vision or plan for these events. This was the case for Shayla.

> Shayla was planning her wedding on a tight budget and informed her mother and soon-to-be mother-in-law that the guest list was limited to fifty people. After they had all agreed on the guest list and the invitations were sent, Shayla's mother-in-law said she felt bad about leaving some friends out, so she invited three more friends and their spouses. Shayla fumed over her mother-in-law's presumptuous behavior. Her own mother had crossed lifelong friends off the guest list, and her mother-in-law did this without consulting her and without offering any financial help.

Have you experienced anything like this? Shayla's response is certainly understandable. Inviting guests to someone else's party is generally in bad form, but when it's your wedding, the boundary violation causes more damage because the event is so special.

Parenting

If you have children, there's a good chance that you've felt like your family or friends have over-stepped their role when it comes to parenting your children. Here are a few examples:

- Giving you unwanted parenting advice

- Ignoring your instructions while watching your children

- Disciplining your children in a way that you disapprove of

- Giving your children gifts, taking your children places, or letting them spend time with people that you've asked them not to

- Telling your children to keep secrets from you

- Dismissing your concerns about your children

- Insisting that they know how to parent your children better than you do

Again, these types of boundary issues come up frequently because people tend to have strong opinions and expectations about how children should be raised, and parents want to protect their children from anything that might be harmful.

Money

How money is handled can elicit strong feelings and be hard to discuss openly with family and friends, especially if there is a large discrepancy in income or wealth. Money boundaries are also challenging because they aren't simply about our right and responsibility to safeguard our financial health. Money can be the vehicle that brings other needs and feelings to the surface, as you'll see in DeShaun's story.

DeShaun feels taken advantage of. His friend Louis never offers to pay when they eat out together or go on a road trip. It's not about the money; DeShaun can afford to cover Louis's meals and travel expenses. The problem is that he feels disrespected and unappreciated because Louis expects DeShaun to pay without asking or thanking him.

Like so many things, thoughts and feelings about money probably stem from your childhood experiences. For example, in some families, money is used to express love. In others, it's used to control people. What messages have you gotten about money?

Consider these questions and use the space below to reflect on your answers:

- What did you learn about spending and saving money from your parents or family?

- Was money a source of comfort and security or a source of conflict and insecurity?

- How did your family view people who struggled financially?

- How did they view those who had lots of financial resources?

- What did you learn about helping those in need?

- What did you learn about asking for financial help?

_____

_____

_____

_____

_____

_____

Becoming more aware of your beliefs about money can help you better understand why you have difficulty setting or accepting boundaries about finances.

Privacy

Privacy creates a physical or emotional space between us and others that allows us to maintain our individuality and share only what feels comfortable or safe. A friend or family member might violate your privacy by asking intrusive questions, looking through your medicine cabinet, or posting an embarrassing photo of you on social media without consent. The need for privacy can vary greatly among people, and if you need significantly more or less privacy than your family and friends, you're likely to experience boundary issues in this area.

Your Boundary Issues with Family and Friends

Now that you've read about some of the most common boundary issues that people have with family and friends, take a few minutes to reflect on the boundary conflicts or differing expectations that you've experienced.

Describe a boundary conflict that you've had with a family member or friend that you haven't been able to resolve.

_____

_____

_____

_____

_____

What have you done to try to resolve this issue?

_____

_____

_____

_____

_____

Even if you haven't been completely successful, pat yourself on the back for trying. Boundary issues with family and friends can be hard to solve because of the emotions and expectations involved. However, knowing what doesn't work can be valuable information that moves you closer to a solution.

Tips for Resolving Boundary Issues with Family and Friends

Now that you've identified the boundary problems that you have with family and friends, you can apply the skills you've been learning throughout this book. Using the Four Steps to Setting Better Boundaries (chapter 4) will help you identify your unmet needs, consider your options, create and implement a plan, and fine-tune your boundaries. However, since boundaries with extended family and friends have some unique challenges, I want to highlight some additional strategies and considerations that you may find helpful.

Respecting Differences

Boundary norms vary greatly among families and cultures, and extended families and groups of friends are becoming increasingly diverse. Your family and friends may have differing religious beliefs, political views, sexual orientations, gender identities, physical abilities, cultural practices, and more. These differences enrich our lives, but they can also contribute to misunderstandings and boundary conflicts if we don't work to understand the beliefs, experiences, and needs of others.

Too often, we assume the worst about others, judge their behavior, and impose our beliefs on them without listening to their perspective and considering alternatives. When we don't understand someone's perspective or culture, we're more likely to feel hurt and angry when they violate our boundaries, and we're more likely to unknowingly violate their boundaries.

Sometimes, it's obvious that you have a different background or culture than someone else, but not always. Households may have norms and traditions that differ from those of their extended family and friends. So, if you're experiencing boundary conflicts with extended family or friends, use the questions that follow to explore ways to understand each other better and find solutions.

Describe a boundary challenge with a family member or friend. What differences may be creating conflict or misunderstandings about boundaries and expectations?

_____

_____

_____

_____

How do you think you've contributed to the conflict or misunderstanding? If you're not sure, are you willing to ask the other person?

_____

_____

_____

_____

How can you get more information to help you understand the other person's beliefs, experiences, and needs?

_____

_____

_____

_____

_____

How can you improve your communication skills to better understand and resolve your differences? (See chapter 5 if you need help.)

_____

_____

_____

_____

_____

How can you show that you're receptive and interested in learning and working together to solve the boundary conflict?

_____

_____

_____

_____

_____

It can be painful to realize that we've been insensitive to someone's culture, made assumptions, or haven't tried hard enough to understand a different perspective. If this is the case for you, try to practice self-forgiveness, because the alternative—feeling shame and guilt—doesn't help us build connections, learn, and compromise.

When I've made a mistake, I find relief by repeating this self-forgiveness mantra.

I forgive myself for my mistakes and shortcomings. I won't be self-critical and unkind to myself because that doesn't benefit anyone. Instead, I will put my energy into treating myself and others with love and respect. I'm committed to learning and growing, so I can better understand others.

Use this space to adapt the mantra or write your own.

_____

_____

_____

_____

_____

_____

Feelings of guilt can create additional barriers to setting boundaries, so we'll talk about how to deal with these feelings in more depth in the next section.

Releasing Guilt

Guilt, the feeling that you've done something wrong, can be a powerful obstacle to setting boundaries. We can feel guilty when setting boundaries with anyone, but guilt tends to be prevalent with our family of origin because we often have static family roles (such as the caretaker or peacemaker) that don't change regardless of our age. And we have rigid ideas about what kind of relationships we should have with our families, how often we should see them, how we should treat them, and how they should treat us. When we don't live up to these roles and expectations, we feel guilty—we think we've done something wrong because we want time apart, have different values, or can't respond to every request for help.

Guilt serves a purpose. When you've actually done something wrong, it's appropriate to feel bad. A moderate amount of guilt can motivate you to do better. But if you have unrealistic expectations of yourself, or others impose impossibly high standards on you, you'll feel guilty even when you haven't done anything wrong. In this case, guilt is a hindrance, not a help. It diminishes self-worth and makes it difficult to assert your needs. If you experience guilt when you try to set boundaries, let's dissect the experience to see what expectations or beliefs are creating those feelings.

Think of a boundary issue or person who tends to elicit feelings of guilt. What's expected of you in this situation or role (parent, child) that's contributing to feelings of guilt?

_____

_____

_____

_____

_____

_____

_____

Using the chart that follows, rate how strongly you and your family members hold these beliefs or expectations. You can substitute a specific family member, such as father or grandma, for the word "family" to personalize this exercise. You can also download a version of this exercise pertaining to friendships from http://www.newharbinger.com/47582.

Belief or Expectation	How strongly do you believe this? (0–10)	How strongly does your family believe this? (0–10)
I should drop everything when my family needs something.		
I should be agreeable and not have conflicts with my family.		
"Blood is thicker than water."		
Children should respect their parents or elders.		
If my family hurts my feelings or mistreats me, I shouldn't make a big deal about it.		
I have to sacrifice my own goals to satisfy my family.		
It's selfish or wrong to set limits with my family.		
I owe my family everything.		
I shouldn't be angry at my family.		
A good _____ (son, mother, etc.) would take care of their family without complaint.		
It's my job to take care of my extended family.		
I should put my extended family's needs before my own.		
It's wrong to cut a family member out of my life.		
I should do whatever it takes to make my family happy.		
I'm a bad _____ (daughter, father, etc.) because _____.		

Notice the beliefs or expectations that you rated a 5 or higher. You may find it helpful to circle them. Choose one to practice releasing guilt with, and write it in the space provided.

Example: I should drop everything when my mother needs something.

_____

_____

Tip   Unrealistic expectations often contain these words:

Must

Should

Always

Never

Everyone

No one

The next step in overcoming feelings of guilt is to challenge the underlying belief or expectation by determining whether it's realistic and makes sense to you. You can do this using the same technique from chapter 3 to challenge fears. The following questions can help you challenge beliefs or expectations that create feelings of guilt:

- Where did this belief or expectation come from?

_____

- Is this *your* belief or expectation or someone else's?

_____

- Is this belief or expectation helpful?

_____

- Does this belief or expectation allow you to care for yourself?

_____

- Would you hold someone else to this same standard?

  _____

- Are there exceptions to these absolutes (always, never)?

  _____

- Who gets to decide what you have to or should do?

  _____

- Does this expectation or belief align with your values?

  _____

Considering your answers to these questions, do you think the belief or expectation that you identified is realistic? Does it make sense to you?

Example: My mother expects me to be on call 24/7, but this isn't realistic because I have my own needs and commitments. I wouldn't expect anyone to be available to me 24/7.

_____

_____

_____

Now, rewrite the belief or expectation so it's more realistic and supportive of your needs.

Example: I can realistically help my mother with some of her needs on the weekends. I believe it's important to balance her needs and mine. I'm still a good daughter even if I say no sometimes.

_____

_____

_____

_____

When you feel confident about your beliefs and expectations, you won't be as susceptible to guilt. However, some people will probably still say that you're wrong because it's been an effective way to get what they want. To prepare for these challenges, write an affirmation or reminder that will help you stay true to your new beliefs. Use these prompts to help you:

I have a right to _____.

I believe _____.

It's okay that I can't please others all the time because _____

_____.

Changing long-held beliefs and expectations takes practice and resolve, but you'll gradually feel less guilty, and this will make it easier for you to set the boundaries you need.

Enlisting Help

Enlisting the help of supportive people can make setting boundaries with family and friends easier. Sometimes, asking for help is simple; sometimes it takes more effort. For example, you may have a best friend who has your back in everything you do. Or you may have a conflict-avoidant partner who doesn't want to get involved.

How do you enlist the help of others? First, it's important to know what kind of help you need. If you ask your brother to back you up when you set boundaries with your mother, he may have a different idea of what it means to "back you up." If neither of you is aware of this difference, you'll both end up frustrated and disappointed. Second, you're more likely to get the help you need when you ask for something specific and determine who in your life is best suited to provide it. So, knowing what you need can help you figure out whom to ask. Here are some examples of how to be specific about the help you need:

- I need help practicing or role-playing setting boundaries.

- I need encouragement, such as a smile, nod, or hand on my shoulder, when I try to set boundaries.

- I need to call or text someone when I feel frustrated with setting boundaries.

- I need a supportive presence, someone to just be in the room with me as a show of support.

- I need a teammate who will set and enforce the same boundaries so the boundary violator can't go around me. (Such as, I need my husband to tell his sister not to smoke in our house and not allow it when I'm not home.)

Take a few minutes now to practice enlisting help.

Identify a boundary issue that you're having with an extended family member or friend.

_____

_____

What kind of help do you need? (Be specific.)

_____

_____

_____

_____

Who is the best person to help you, and why?

_____

_____

_____

_____

Asking for help can be a great tool when setting boundaries with anyone in your life, not just extended family members and friends. However, it's often in these close, personal relationships that we need or expect help from others. This tends to be especially true of our partners. Here are some specific tools for enlisting your partner's help.

WORK COOPERATIVELY WITH YOUR PARTNER

For many couples, setting boundaries with extended family is a major source of conflict. It could be that your partner doesn't want to get involved, or they may actively undermine your efforts to set boundaries. In either case, it's hard to set and enforce boundaries with extended family without the cooperation and support of your partner. However, when you consider what you both need, are willing to compromise, and have empathy for each other, you can set boundaries that work for both of you.

One of the challenges of setting boundaries with extended family is that you each have different relationships with your families—and, consequently, different needs. It's common for people to feel closer and more connected to their own family than their partner's. For example, you may find your mother-in-law's insults intolerable, but your husband may be unfazed by her behavior. You want your husband to ask her to stop or reinforce a boundary you've established, but he enjoys his mother's company and doesn't understand why you're so upset. Collaborating on a boundary issue such as this is complex because you're dealing with what you need from your mother-in-law and, simultaneously, what you need from your partner. To address both needs, you can adapt the strategies from chapters 6 and 8 to communicate your needs and feelings and work toward compromise.

Describe a boundary issue that you have with a family member for which you'd like your partner's support.

_____

_____

_____

_____

_____

What do you need from your extended family member? Be sure to focus on your unmet need, not on the behavior change that you want from your family member.

Example: I need to feel respected by my mother-in-law.

_____

What do you need from your partner?

Example: I need to feel loved and valued by my husband.

_____

Try using an I-statement to communicate your feelings and needs to your partner.

Example: I feel hurt when your mother insults me, and I'd like you to ask her to stop and enforce consequences if she won't. Is that something you're willing to help me with?

I feel _____ when _____,

and I'd like _____.

Is that something you're willing to help me with?

    If your partner agrees, you now have an opportunity to negotiate what the help will entail, when it will be given, and so forth.

    Often, the most painful part of such an experience is not having had your partner's support. So, again, an I-statement is a good way to communicate this to your partner.

Example: I feel hurt when you don't say anything to your mother when she insults me. I feel like you care more about her feelings than mine, and I'd like you to acknowledge my feelings and stand up for me. Is that something you're willing to do?

I feel _____ when _____,

and I'd like _____.

Is that something you're willing to do?

    Communicating your feelings can help your partner empathize with your experiences. And sharing your needs, and being interested in your partner's needs, will help you work toward meaningful compromises so you'll both feel supported and understood.

Summary

In this chapter, we explored common boundary struggles with extended family and friends and how to respect differences, release feelings of guilt that impede our boundaries, and ask for help. Now you'll learn skills to set boundaries with the most difficult people in your life.

Chapter 11

Boundary Skills with Difficult People

Is there someone in your life who consistently challenges your boundaries and disrespects you? This is such a draining, discouraging, and infuriating experience that you may lash out against such individuals with anger and demands, or you may have stopped trying to set boundaries with them because it feels hopeless or scary. But you're not powerless, and in this chapter, you'll learn why it's important to recognize "difficult people" and how to approach setting boundaries with them.

Recognizing Difficult People

Sometimes even when we do everything right—use assertive communication skills, are clear about what we need, and make requests, not demands—we still can't seem to set effective boundaries with certain people. When this happens, you may be dealing with someone whom I'd characterize as a "difficult person."

Although there are no official criteria, difficult people typically:

- Act entitled and think rules don't apply to them.

- Manipulate others to get what they want.

- Repeatedly violate boundaries.

- Don't consider other people's feelings or needs.

- Blame others and don't take responsibility for their actions.

- Make unreasonable demands.

- Refuse to compromise.

- Always have to be right.

- Yell, curse, criticize, and name-call when they don't get their way.

- Can be volatile, unpredictable, or physically aggressive.

- Lie frequently.

- Use passive-aggressive behavior (such as the silent treatment, "forgetting," or criticism disguised as a compliment).

- Gossip or speak ill of people behind their backs.

- Play the victim.

- Gaslight (a form of manipulation that makes you doubt your perception of reality).

- Undermine your relationship with your spouse, kids, or others.

- Belittle your values, beliefs, and choices.

- Lack genuine concern or interest in you and your life.

- Expect you to help them but don't return the favor.

- Rarely apologize, and if they do, it's shallow, coerced, or fake.

- May struggle with addiction or other problems, but don't want to change.

The following examples illustrate what it's like to deal with a difficult person.

Amir's father brings his dog, Buster, almost everywhere. And although the dog bit Amir a few years ago, he never objected when his dad brought Buster to his house. But now that Amir has a new baby, he doesn't want an aggressive dog around. So, he politely and calmly told his father that he can no longer bring Buster when he visits. Amir thought this was an understandable boundary, but his father responded with anger. "You're not going to tell me what to do, Amir!" His father got inches from his face and was yelling, "I'm your father and you'll listen to me! I don't care what you want! You've always been a crybaby!" His father's tirade continued for a full five minutes. Then, he sat down on Amir's sofa and put his feet up as if nothing had happened.

Every Friday night, Ruth's husband, Nigel, comes home with two cases of beer and a bottle of whiskey. He holes up in the basement all weekend, drinking, watching pornography, and playing video games. Ruth has begged him to stop, given ultimatums and lectures, and hidden his booze. But Nigel insists he doesn't have a problem and won't discuss it. Ruth ends up spending the weekend entertaining Nigel's son from a previous relationship and cleaning up beer cans, half-eaten plates of food, and cigarette butts.

Difficult people can make our lives miserable. They often try to convince us that our boundaries are unreasonable or that we're mean, unfair, or irrational. However, when someone doesn't respect our boundaries, it doesn't mean that we're asking too much or shouldn't set boundaries. Other people's inability or unwillingness to respect our boundaries usually reflects their difficulty with self-management or empathy, not that our needs or boundaries are wrong.

If there's someone in your life whom you suspect is a difficult person, answer the following questions as you reflect on your experiences with them.

How does this person respond to your boundaries? Has their behavior made you reluctant to set boundaries?

_____

_____

_____

_____

_____

Usually, a difficult person's behavior makes them easy to spot, like Nigel and Amir's father. But some difficult people are quite charming (at least some of the time) and good at convincing us that their behavior is normal or that they'll change. However, if you notice your thoughts, feelings, and body sensations, they'll usually alert you when you're dealing with a difficult person. For example, you might think, *I hate spending time with Eli,* or *I better clean up before my mother arrives and tells me I'm a slob.* You might feel anxious, angry, exhausted, or depressed. And you might notice that your heart is pounding, your hands are shaking, you get more headaches, or you can't sleep.

It's helpful to become aware of how your mind and body respond to difficult people so you can take steps to care for and protect yourself. Before answering the following questions, you may need to pay attention to your thoughts, feelings, and body sensations for several days or weeks and then record your answers.

What thoughts do you have when you interact with or anticipate interacting with this person?

_____

_____

_____

_____

_____

How do you feel?

_____

_____

_____

_____

_____

How does your body respond?

_____

_____

_____

_____

_____

How else are you negatively affected by this person?

_____

_____

_____

_____

_____

Even if you're not sure whether someone in your life is truly difficult, reading and doing the exercises in the rest of this chapter will give you greater clarity and additional boundary-setting skills that you'll find useful.

Tips for Setting Boundaries with Difficult People

When dealing with difficult people, we need to take a different approach to setting boundaries than we do with most people. Strategies such as trying to compromise or sharing our feelings won't work. Instead, we need to focus on being safe, avoiding power struggles, and knowing what we can control. Otherwise, we'll get stuck in unproductive conversations that deteriorate into arguments, blaming, ultimatums, or worse.

Prioritize Safety

When deciding how to deal with a difficult person, safety must be your priority. Don't underestimate the harm that a difficult person can cause.

Although no one can definitively predict another person's behavior, past behavior is usually a strong indicator of future behavior. It's important not to minimize the dangerous things this person has done or the ways he or she has harmed you or others.

If you feel comfortable, note this person's dangerous or harmful behaviors. Seeing them in writing can help you overcome any lingering denial. Or you can write this list somewhere more secure, or just make a mental note if you don't feel safe writing it.

_____

_____

_____

_____

_____

It can be painful to fully acknowledge the harm a friend or loved one has caused, so be gentle with yourself and keep working on this chapter at whatever pace feels right to you.

To make safety a priority for you (and your children, if you have any), consider proactive things you can do, such as the safety tips listed here:

- You don't need to explain or justify your boundaries to difficult people. Doing so can make matters worse. Difficult people will pick apart your reasons and use them to criticize and invalidate your needs. If communicating a boundary or consequence is likely to anger someone and put you in danger, take action to protect yourself without explanation. This might include leaving the situation, calling the police, or moving out.

- If someone has been violent, aggressive, or threatened you or others, have potentially upsetting conversations in a public place or with another adult present.

- If you don't feel safe communicating in person, use text, email, or phone.

- Consider getting a restraining order if someone has been aggressive or threatened you or others.

- Create a safety plan that includes identifying a safe place that you can go, phone numbers of supportive people and community resources (such as shelters and crisis lines), cash, and identification. You can also find a list of domestic violence and crisis resources in the Resources page at http://www.newharbinger.com/47582.

What steps can you take to protect yourself from harm?

_____

_____

_____

_____

_____

No one wants to think about needing a safety plan or restraining order—and hopefully you won't—but it's better to be prepared. You may not be used to putting yourself first in this way, and it can be really hard to do so. You'll get there by making small changes, and prioritizing your safety is the first step.

Avoid Power Struggles

Difficult people want to be in control. They often argue and create conflicts to avoid accountability and distract us from setting and enforcing boundaries. Since difficult people thrive on conflict, it falls on us to avoid power struggles.

Arguing, or even negotiating, with someone who isn't interested in understanding you or lacks empathy won't be productive. Try to see this for what it is—a distraction—and don't take the bait. Difficult people know just the right accusation or triggering event to bring up to get your blood boiling, so it's challenging to recognize when someone's trying to pull you into an argument. With practice, you'll learn to notice when this is happening and avoid reacting.

How do difficult people pull you into power struggles or arguments? What do they say or do that consistently upsets you and causes you to react?

_____

_____

_____

_____

These are the behaviors that you need to be on the lookout for. The harder part, of course, is changing your response.

What can you do instead of arguing, defending yourself, yelling, being sarcastic, or making demands? Try to list as many options as you can. If you have trouble with this, think about what someone else—a specific person you admire or an imaginary person who is wise, calm, and self-confident—would do.

_____

_____

_____

_____

_____

This is a great start! Knowing your triggers and creating a plan to respond differently will help you avoid power struggles. This will take a lot of effort on your part because difficult people are masters at drawing others into arguments. But don't give up; difficult people will persist in trying to bait you for a long time, but many will eventually stop if they can't control you and get the reaction they're looking for.

We also need to be careful that we don't create power struggles by being controlling ourselves. Many of us have mistakenly used boundaries to try to get others to do what we want. Usually, we mean well—we want our alcoholic parents to stop drinking and our still-living-at-home adult children to get jobs—but we can't force people, especially difficult people, to change. Repeatedly nagging and hounding them can lead to power struggles.

How do you contribute to power struggles by forcing your agenda?

_____

_____

_____

_____

_____

Difficult people don't want to change. When we accept this and stop trying to get them to change, we can focus on what we can control and get our needs met in another way.

Focus on What You Can Control

The only way to set boundaries with difficult people is to focus on what you can control. For the most part, difficult people won't comply with requests to change their behavior. They'll respond with anger (like Amir's father), deny there's a problem (like Nigel), play the victim, agree to change but never follow through, or even laugh in your face and walk away. Whatever the response, it's unlikely to be a sincere attempt to change. The more you reason, plead, or threaten, the more defensive, angry, or manipulative the difficult person will become. This leaves you with one choice—do what's in your power to improve your life.

Accepting that we can't get others to change can be frustrating, but the good news is that we can get many of our needs met by changing our own thoughts and behaviors. Most of us don't have much practice with setting boundaries through personal change. Perhaps we underestimate its effectiveness, or we genuinely think we can help someone by convincing them to change, or we'd just prefer that others do the difficult work of changing themselves. Let's practice a bit so you'll feel more comfortable identifying what you alone can do to set the boundaries you need.

Look back at Amir's story. His father is unlikely to change no matter how nicely Amir asks or how many valid reasons he provides. How can Amir set and enforce his boundary if his father continues to bring his dog? What's in Amir's control?

_____

_____

_____

_____

_____

Now, consider a situation from your own life. How is a difficult person violating one of your boundaries? For this exercise, think about one specific boundary violation.

_____

_____

_____

_____

_____

What personal needs are you trying to meet with this boundary?

_____

Assuming the difficult person behaves exactly as they have in the past, what can you do to get your needs met? Brainstorm as many options as possible regardless of whether they're "good" options.

_____

_____

_____

_____

_____

It is likely that none of Amir's or your options are ideal. For example, it would be difficult for Amir not to invite his father to his home or to refuse to open the door if he brings his dog. However, these are two things he *can* do to protect his child from his father's dog. Difficult people often leave us with few choices for setting and enforcing boundaries, which is why we may choose to accept imperfect solutions.

Accept Imperfect Solutions

In an ideal world, people would enthusiastically embrace our boundaries and understand our needs and feelings, but this is a fantasy when dealing with difficult people. Because they refuse to change or compromise, we often need to make difficult choices and do things that feel harsh or unloving, such as limiting or ending contact with them, but that are truly in our best interest.

Regardless, it's hard to accept that some people won't respect us or our boundaries. And even when we focus on what we can control, they may try to sabotage our boundaries with guilt, bullying, and belittling. This is another power play commonly used by difficult people to try to control us. They think that if they make us feel bad enough about setting limits, we'll back down and they'll be able to do whatever they want.

Here again, it helps to be prepared for this type of response, to recognize it as manipulation, and to name it as such: *Eli is using guilt to try to control me* or *Eli is using verbal abuse to try to manipulate me into giving him money for alcohol.* (*Important note:* Only make these statements to yourself or write them down somewhere you're assured of privacy. Directly calling a difficult person out on their manipulative behavior will cause conflict or further abuse; it won't result in the person taking responsibility or changing.)

Don't sugarcoat a difficult person's behavior. You need to name the behavior for what it is: control, manipulation, and abuse. Doing this makes it clear that their behavior is unacceptable, not your fault, and not something you can change. Seeing harmful behavior for what it is can help you accept an imperfect solution, such as getting a divorce or not allowing your children to visit their grandparents.

Imperfect solutions often involve giving up something we wanted or were familiar with in order to have something we need more. For example, leaving an abusive partner can mean losing an important relationship with someone you love in order to have the safety you need. It's a significant loss, and you aren't going to immediately feel better because this difficult person is gone. Instead, you'll probably feel conflicted—sad, guilty, angry, relieved. Grieving the end of a relationship, or accepting any imperfect solution, is a process that includes remembering why you made this decision, accepting your feelings, finding healthy outlets for your feelings, and treating yourself with kindness.

When you're wrestling with an imperfect solution, remember:

- Why this boundary matters to you.

    Example: This boundary matters because I need to keep my son safe.

- You have the right to set boundaries.

    Example: I have the right to decide who or what comes into my home.

    _____

- When other people respond unfavorably, it doesn't mean you've done something wrong.

    Example: My father's anger doesn't mean I've done something wrong.

    _____

- You're not responsible for how other people feel about your boundaries or how they respond.

    Example: My father's feelings and actions aren't my responsibility. It's not my job to make him feel better.

    _____

I also encourage you to increase your self-care—get enough sleep, exercise, spend time with supportive people, or enjoy a hobby—whenever you're struggling with your boundaries or going through a big change. A therapist can also be an important ally when dealing with difficult people. They can provide a safe space to process your feelings, identify options, and work toward accepting imperfect solutions.

Summary

Difficult people make setting boundaries very challenging! Assertive communication, negotiating, making requests, and many of the other boundary-setting skills you've learned rarely work. But once you recognize that you're dealing with a difficult person, you can take a different approach that prioritizes safety, avoids power struggles, focuses on what you can control, and accepts imperfect solutions. Now that we've focused on setting boundaries with others, we'll turn to part four, where we'll learn about setting boundaries with ourselves.

Part Four

PRACTICING BOUNDARY SKILLS WITH YOURSELF

Chapter 12

Respecting Other People's Boundaries

Up until this point, we've been talking about asserting our needs and setting boundaries with other people. Now, we're shifting to look at the boundaries or limits we need to set with ourselves. In this chapter, we'll discuss the importance of respecting other people's boundaries.

Boundaries Are a Two-Way Street

As I've noted throughout this book, boundaries are the foundation of healthy relationships. But they don't just apply to other people. Boundaries go both ways—and we can't expect others to respect our boundaries if we don't respect theirs.

This, of course, is easier said than done. We don't always like other people's boundaries; we don't like being told no or having to compromise. But if we can't respect other people's boundaries, our relationships will suffer. We'll be frequently frustrated and annoyed, we'll have more arguments, and ultimately, people won't want to be around us. When we respect other people's boundaries, we accept their right to self-determination, to do what's right for themselves. This builds trust and emotional safety because others are more likely to be open and honest with us if they experience us as respectful and nonjudgmental.

Ways We Violate Other People's Boundaries

We all violate other people's boundaries from time to time. Often, these violations are minor infractions or accidents—you sit too close to someone on the subway and they slide over, indicating discomfort, or you accidentally open a piece of your partner's mail.

However, we all violate bigger boundaries, too. And it's the violations that cause harm, or that are done with a desire to control or punish, that most need our attention. So, these are the boundary violations we'll focus on in this chapter.

You may disrespect other people's boundaries by:

- Invalidating their feelings or opinions.

    Example: *Just get over it. It's not a big deal.*

- Using guilt or passive-aggressive behavior to control others.

    Examples: *You use your roommate's shampoo out of spite because she had a condescending tone when she asked you not to use it.*

    You complain about how lonely you are, so your daughter will visit.

- Acting in an overly familiar way.

    Examples: *You tell a woman you just met in the checkout line all about your health problems.*

    You leave the bathroom door open when you use the toilet at your son and daughter-in-law's house.

- Breaking trust.

    Example: *You tell your mother something your brother shared with you in confidence.*

- Giving unwanted advice.

    Example: *Your best friend confides in you about his girlfriend's infidelity. You tell him cheating is a deal breaker and he should end the relationship because it will only get worse.*

- Being pushy; trying to convince someone to do something they don't want to do.

    Examples: *You badger your friend to have another cookie even though she said she'd had enough.*

    During an argument, your wife says she needs some space and is going to walk around the block and will be back in fifteen minutes. You respond, "No. We have to keep talking about this. You can't just walk out in the middle of an argument."

- Being aggressive or hurtful.

    Examples: *You block the exit so your wife can't leave.*

    Your roommate confronts you about using her shampoo; you tell her she's selfish and slam the door.

Do any of these behaviors sound familiar? We all overstep sometimes, but even knowing this, it can be hard to admit how often we do and how much damage it causes. However, I encourage you to take an honest look at your behavior, because awareness is the first step to change.

Briefly describe one or two occasions when you've disrespected someone's boundaries.

_____

_____

_____

_____

_____

_____

In what ways have your relationships been negatively affected because you didn't respect others' boundaries?

_____

_____

_____

_____

As you reflect on these experiences, try to appreciate them as learning opportunities; when you recognize your mistakes, you can learn to do better. Judging yourself harshly isn't productive. It leads to shame, not growth. Most of us struggle to respect other people's boundaries, and it's not because we're bad people, but because we don't yet have the awareness and skills we need.

Why It's So Hard to Accept Other People's Boundaries

What goes through your mind when someone tells you no? You might feel angry; it's frustrating to not get what you want. Or you might feel ashamed, like you're being scolded for doing something wrong or asking for too much. Some people also feel afraid because being told no stirs up memories or fears of being rejected or abandoned. Hearing "no" is surprisingly difficult, regardless of how old or mature you are, because it can bring up a lot of difficult feelings.

How do you feel when someone sets a limit that you don't like or tells you no?

_____

_____

_____

_____

How do you usually behave in such a situation?

_____

_____

_____

_____

You may notice that how you feel about other people's boundaries depends on who's setting the boundary, what the boundary is, and how it's set. For example, it may be very painful when your father hangs up on you, but you aren't particularly bothered when your friend says he needs to get off the phone because he's busy. What's the difference? It could be that your father has a history of rejecting you and is harsh in his approach, whereas your friend uses a polite tone of voice and usually calls back when he's available to talk. If this was your experience, it's easy to understand why one boundary is more painful than the other.

But what often happens is we unconsciously carry the pain and anger of being rejected or hurt by one person with us into our relationships with others. When this happens, we may find unrelated boundaries set by different people painful as well. For example, if you experience your friend's boundary as hurtful even though he was polite and gentle and has never rejected you, it may be subconsciously reactivating painful feelings related to your father's behavior.

When you find someone's boundary very painful, despite having no evidence that they're impinging on your rights, be curious about your reaction: Does the experience remind you of something from the past? Have you felt like this when people have set limits with you before? You may have to look back to your childhood to make these connections.

Think of a boundary that's particularly painful for you. Does your reaction to this boundary seem justified? If not, can you think of how this boundary might be connected to a past experience?

_____

_____

_____

_____

_____

Even if you can't figure out exactly where your intense feelings are coming from, it can be helpful to recognize that they're normal and your body's way of alerting you to a situation that was painful in the past. This allows you to notice what's different in this situation and look for signs that this person and their boundaries aren't a threat. When you don't perceive others as a threat, it's much easier to respect their boundaries.

How to Respect Other People's Boundaries

Respecting boundaries doesn't mean we necessarily agree with other people's decisions or opinions; it means we accept their right to make those decisions and have their opinions. Respecting boundaries also doesn't mean doing everything someone asks or demands; we can respectfully decline a request and thereby set our own boundary. And respecting someone's boundaries doesn't mean tolerating abuse or being passive. Our goal is to respect others *and* respect ourselves. Let's now review some tips for respecting other people's boundaries.

Ask Rather Than Assume

Asking for more information can help us avoid many boundary violations because we're more likely to overstep boundaries when we don't understand someone's needs or viewpoint. When we don't have enough information to understand another person or situation, our brain automatically fills in the missing pieces to make sense of what's going on. As a result, we make assumptions about other people's needs and motives. We misconstrue their tone of voice, facial expressions, and behavior because we're making assumptions based on our own experiences, beliefs, and feelings. We're especially prone to making assumptions when we're rushed, stressed, have had prior conflicts with someone, or have vastly different life experiences.

I'll use Jane and Cal's story to illustrate how assumptions can lead to boundary violations, and how to ask for more information to avoid this problem.

> *After dating for a year, Jane and Cal are having relationship problems. During a heated argument, Cal says, "Let's take some time apart." Jane's not sure what he means. So, two days later she calls Cal and he's furious that she didn't respect his request for space.*

We can ask clarifying questions to try to get the information we need when boundaries and expectations aren't clear. Here are some things Jane could say:

- I want to respect your boundaries and give you the time you need. What's the best way for me to do that?

- I'm concerned that I don't understand. Can you explain more about what you need?

- How much time do you think you'll need?

- To me, taking some time apart means no contact for a day or two. Is that what you have in mind?

- Is it okay for me to contact you on social media?

- I don't want to overstep, so I'd like to know specifically what you do and don't want me to do.

The answers to any of these questions will help Jane understand more about Cal's boundaries.

Your clarifying questions will vary depending on the situation, but in general, you want clear answers to the following questions:

- Who is being asked to do something?

- What are they being asked to do?

- Where will it take place?

- When will it be done?

- How long will it last?

- How will it be done?

Identify a situation where you violated someone's boundaries. What clarifying questions would have helped you understand and avoid disrespecting their boundaries?

_____

_____

_____

_____

_____

It's not always easy to ask clarifying questions; some people get angry and defensive when asked or may turn your request for information into an insult. Do your best to use a warm tone of voice and express genuine interest in understanding and respecting their boundaries. Sharing the feelings and needs that are prompting your questions (such as *I'm confused* or *I want to understand*) can also create emotional safety and avoid the sense that you're grilling the other person (Rosenberg 2003). However, if someone refuses to explain what they need, it's hard to respect their boundaries because we aren't mind readers! In this case, respect their boundaries as well as you can with the information you have, and remember that boundaries work best when everyone is willing to fully participate in the process.

Listen Attentively

In addition to asking questions, we need to be good listeners, which means being attentive to what's being said and how it's being said. Make sure you're giving others your full attention, because it's respectful and you're bound to miss part of their message if you're looking at your phone or thinking about what you're going to say next. Also, allow the other person to finish speaking before you respond.

Be Caring and Considerate

Perhaps the most important thing you can do to respect someone's boundaries is to convey that you care and are interested in what they need. Here are some examples of phrases you can use to do this:

- I want to understand what you need.

- I care about you and your needs.

- Can we talk more about this?

- I'm not always able to meet your needs or do what you want, but I do care about you.

- Let's see if we can compromise.

- We don't have to agree on everything to be friends.

- I respect your opinion even though I disagree.

- I don't want to overstep.

- _____

- _____

- _____

Care and consideration can also be shown with a warm facial expression, gentle tone of voice, relaxed body posture, and attentiveness.

Take No for an Answer

Sometimes, the most respectful response is to accept somebody's *no* without asking why or trying to change their mind. Pushing someone to explain their no, even if our intention is to be helpful or accommodating, can put them on the spot and force an uncomfortable, hurtful, or embarrassing explanation that they didn't want to give. This is especially true with people we're not close to, like coworkers and acquaintances. Instead, we can take no for an answer and trust that if someone wants to give an explanation or ask us to make a change, they will.

Don't Take It Personally

When we take other people's boundaries personally, we perceive them as personal attacks or as ways to disconnect from or punish us. None of that feels good! And understandably, when we experience others' boundaries this way, we're inclined to push back, resist their boundaries, and try to convince them that their boundaries are wrong or unnecessary. But doing so is fundamentally disrespectful, and it doesn't build the connection we crave.

Instead, we can notice when we're over-personalizing a boundary. Over-personalizing is caused by distorted thoughts and negative beliefs about ourselves. Being aware of these unhelpful thoughts helps us change them.

Identify a boundary that you're taking personally.

Example: Sam said he doesn't want me to put my feet on him when we're lying on the couch.

_____

How do you feel about this boundary?

Example: I feel hurt and worried.

_____

Identify the specific thought or belief that makes this boundary difficult for you to accept.

Example: I think Sam doesn't like being close to me.

_____

Use the list of cognitive distortions available at http://www.newharbinger.com/47582 to see whether this is a distorted thought. If so, what kind?

Example: Overgeneralizing, mind reading.

_____

Next, look for and record evidence that supports or refutes the accuracy of this thought. Use the questions available at http://www.newharbinger.com/47582 to help you challenge your distorted thought.

Example: I'm making assumptions about what Sam thinks and overgeneralizing based on this one situation. Maybe he just doesn't like feet. We hug and kiss often and he doesn't object to being close in other ways.

_____

_____

_____

_____

_____

Now, rewrite your thought or belief as a more accurate and supportive statement.

Example: Sam and I are close. Asking me to move my feet doesn't change that.

_____

_____

_____

This exercise can help you change the distorted thoughts that cause you to take things personally and replace them with thoughts that are more accurate and supportive, which can help you respect other people's boundaries.

What to Do If You Violate Someone's Boundaries

Hopefully, if you use the tips we just discussed, you won't often violate other people's boundaries. However, we're all human, and sometimes we make mistakes. When we violate other people's boundaries, it's important to apologize and change our behavior.

Making a Good Apology

Making a good apology, one that satisfies the person who was wronged, is more complicated than you might think. Researchers (Lewicki, Polin, and Lount 2016) identified six components of an effective apology:

1. Acknowledgment of responsibility

2. Offer of repair

3. Expression of regret

4. Explanation of what went wrong

5. Declaration of repentance

6. Request for forgiveness

Ideally, you'll use all these components when apologizing, at least for major boundary violations. However, the research showed that the components aren't equally important. The most important component is taking responsibility or acknowledging that you were at fault. The second most important element is offering a repair or being willing to take action to make things right. So, you'll want to make sure that your apologies include at least these two elements.

Here's an example of an apology that takes responsibility and offers a repair: *I regret drinking before Dad's funeral and disrupting the service. It's my fault. I take responsibility for the pain I caused you and I want to make things right. I'm going to AA meetings regularly so I can stay sober and avoid hurting you again. Is there something else I can do to repair the damage?*

This is an example of an inadequate apology that doesn't take responsibility and doesn't offer a repair: *I'm sorry if you were upset that I had a few drinks before Dad's funeral. I didn't think you'd care.*

Giving a thorough and heartfelt apology isn't something most of us are skilled at doing. As you can see, it involves more than the basic "I'm sorry." An insincere apology that blames the victim or invalidates their feelings (like the second example) can cause more harm. But, if you practice, crafting an effective apology gets easier.

Practice writing an apology for a boundary you've disrespected.

_____

_____

_____

_____

_____

_____

_____

_____

Changing Your Behavior

Lewicki and his colleagues' research also tells us that, when possible, we need to repair the damage we caused and learn to do better in the future. Apologies don't mean much, even sincere ones, if we continue to disrespect other people's boundaries. We need to change our behavior.

Take some time to think about the changes you need to make. Which of the tips mentioned earlier in this chapter (ask rather than assume, listen attentively, demonstrate care and concern, take no for an answer, and don't take things personally) do you need to work on? There may be other behavioral changes that you need to make, such as not using drugs or alcohol that impair your judgment, going to therapy, taking medication, or getting more sleep. Consider all the factors that affect your mood, self-control, ability to communicate effectively, and ability to stay calm and present-focused.

What changes do you need to make to improve your ability to respect other people's boundaries? Be as specific as possible. For example, instead of *I need to listen better*, identify a specific aspect of listening that you want to improve, such as *I need to put my phone away when talking with Kai.*

_____

_____

_____

_____

_____

How will you make these changes? What resources or help do you need?

_____

_____

_____

_____

_____

Identifying what you need to change is a great start and making a plan to do so creates actionable steps to make the changes a reality. However, even when you're highly motivated, behavior change doesn't happen all at once. It can be helpful to let others know that you're working on making changes. For example, if you've violated one of your wife's boundaries by constantly interrupting her, you could say something like, "I'm working on improving my listening skills by giving you my full attention and not interrupting so I can better understand and respect your boundaries." This is another way to show someone that you're serious about making changes and that they matter to you.

Summary

It takes courage to admit when you've disrespected someone's boundaries, but to create and sustain mature and satisfying relationships you need to be able to acknowledge your mistakes, apologize, and change your behavior. I hope you're now more aware of how you violate other people's boundaries, understand that you're not the only one who struggles with this, and have additional skills to avoid doing so. In the next chapter, we'll work on setting boundaries with ourselves so we can manage our behavior more effectively.

Chapter 13

Boundaries as Self-Management

Most of us struggle to manage some aspects of our behavior, such as our spending habits, drinking, or social media use. Throughout this book, we've talked about how hard it is to say no to other people, and it can be equally tough to say no to ourselves. In this chapter, we'll discuss how you can improve your life by setting boundaries with yourself and how to do this in a way that motivates and respects yourself.

Why You Need to Set Boundaries with Yourself

What would happen if you let yourself eat a pint of ice cream in front of the television every night or called your ex-partner whenever you felt lonely? To stay physically and emotionally healthy, reach our goals, and live according to our values, we need to set limits with ourselves. Boundaries are rules or guidelines that inform our choices. They make it easier for us to resist temptation, form healthy habits, and make decisions that support our goals and values.

See if you can relate to Tessa's struggles with self-management.

At 7:36 a.m., Tessa finally turns off her alarm and gets out of bed. After pushing the snooze button four times, she's running late. There's no time to exercise. She scans her closet for something suitable to wear and finds nothing. So, she sifts through piles of dirty laundry and finds her favorite pants behind the bathroom door. Having skipped breakfast, Tessa's starving by midmorning. She buys a latte and muffin at the coffee shop and immediately feels frustrated because she didn't stick to her budget or her plan to cut back on sugar.

If Tessa could set limits for herself and stick to them, it would be easier for her to get up on time, exercise, keep up with the laundry, stick to her budget, and eat healthfully. And being able to do these things would likely make her feel better physically and mentally; she'd have more energy and feel less stressed and more accomplished. Setting boundaries with yourself creates structure and predictability, which keep your life running smoothly, so you can be productive, stay healthy, and feel good about your choices.

How do you think setting limits with yourself can improve your life?

_____

_____

_____

Of course, managing our behavior and setting limits for ourselves isn't easy or fun. But, as you can tell from Tessa's example, and by thinking about your life, there are many benefits.

Self-Management Is Learned

Before we delve into how to set boundaries with yourself, I want to stress the importance of not judging yourself for a lack of self-management. Everyone struggles with self-management to some extent. It's not a personal failing! We aren't born with self-discipline; it's a set of skills that we must learn and practice throughout our lives.

Your parents or caregivers were your first and most influential teachers. As we've discussed, if your parents didn't create structure and boundaries for you (and themselves), or they did it inconsistently, you probably didn't develop healthy habits and routines or learn how to set limits for yourself. The same can also be true if your parents had harsh, rigid rules and expectations because their need for control didn't allow you to practice self-management, to learn through trial and error; your parents were managing your behavior rather than teaching you how to manage it yourself. Also, consider what you learned by observing how your parents managed their own behavior. Did your parents model healthy habits, moderation, and a reasonably consistent schedule? Or did they drink excessively, sleep all day, and fail to pay the bills on time? These observations can make a lasting impression.

For those who didn't learn self-management skills in childhood, it's common to swing back and forth between being too lenient with yourself (*I deserve another scoop of ice cream*) and too harsh or critical (*I'm so fat; I'm never going to eat ice cream again*). Our goal is to find a middle ground—the ability to compassionately hold ourselves accountable and improve our self-management, but not expect ourselves to do it perfectly, because that's impossible.

How to Set Boundaries with Yourself

There are three steps to setting boundaries with yourself: 1) identify areas of your life that need better self-management, 2) create goals to change your behavior, and 3) be kind to yourself when you make a mistake. Let's start with step 1.

Step 1: Identify Areas of Your Life That Need Better Self-Management

We all have areas of our lives that we don't manage very well. You may already be aware of specific areas that need more structure and limits, or you may only have a general sense that you're not as disciplined as you'd like. Use this list of common self-management struggles to help you identify your own.

Managing your finances. Issues include overspending, late payments, debt, loaning money that isn't repaid, not saving money for a particular goal (retirement, vacation, education), and not filing taxes.

Managing your time. Issues include overscheduling yourself, being late, not prioritizing important activities, procrastinating, not completing tasks, working too much, and staying up too late.

Managing your health. Issues include under- or overeating, smoking, excessive alcohol or drug use, lack of exercise, not managing a chronic health problem or taking prescribed medication, not getting enough sleep, and risky behavior, such as unsafe sex or not wearing a seatbelt.

Managing your relationships. Issues involve mistreating others or continuing relationships with people who cause you physical or emotional pain.

Managing your thoughts and emotions. Issues include ruminating about problems, self-criticism, untreated depression, anxiety, or other mental health concerns.

Managing your environment. Issues include not cleaning or doing laundry, not completing home maintenance projects, clutter, and disorganization.

Take some time to reflect on what areas of your life need more structure or limits. What behaviors feel out of control or unpredictable, or create problems for you?

_____

_____

_____

_____

_____

Use this chart to record the specific behaviors that you want to change, their negative effects, and how motivated you are to change them. You may want to do this over several days to give yourself time to identify a variety of self-management struggles.

Specific Issue	Negative Effects	Motivation Level (1–10)
Example: Staying up late	Tired, irritable, trouble getting up, late for work	8

Trying to address all our self-management issues at once can be overwhelming. People usually get the best results when they focus on one change or goal at a time. So, start with the behavior that's causing you the most problems and that you're highly motivated to change.

What behavior do you want to change first?

_____

Now that you've identified an area of your life that needs better self-management, it's time to create a structured plan for setting limits with yourself.

Step 2: Set Goals to Change Your Behavior

If you're like me, you've probably tried many times to change your bad habits and become more disciplined. Your struggle with self-management isn't because you lack willpower or are incapable. Often, the problem is that you *thought* about changing, but didn't create a concrete, realistic plan and see it through.

SMART goals are a simple and popular tool for setting goals; you may already be familiar with the concept. SMART is an acronym for specific, measurable, achievable, relevant, time-bound. Here's how we can apply it to self-management.

Specific: What specifically do you want to accomplish?

Nonspecific goal: I'm going to eat healthfully.

Specific goal: I'm going to eat five servings of vegetables every day.

Which goal do you think is more useful and likely to be accomplished? "Eating healthfully" can mean many things—not eating fast food, eliminating sugar, eating more vegetables, or drinking a protein shake for breakfast. Any of these activities might improve your health, but they're hard to accomplish when the goal is so broad. In contrast, when you specify that you're going to focus on one particular action, like eating vegetables, you're more likely to follow through.

Narrowing your focus is a good start, but the more specific you can be, the better prepared you'll be and the greater the likelihood of success. You might ask yourself: *How will I incorporate vegetables into my diet? What vegetables will I eat? When will I prepare them?*

Here's an example of an even more specific goal: *I'll eat five servings of vegetables every day; one for breakfast, two for lunch, and two for dinner. On Sundays, I'll go to the farmers' market and buy vegetables for the week. I'll make a large salad to eat as part of my lunch throughout the week.*

Measurable: How will you know when you've achieved your goal? Measuring the outcome will tell you whether you've accomplished what you set out to do. It also helps you be specific. Notice the difference between these goals:

My goal is to exercise.

My goal is to exercise more.

My goal is to exercise for thirty minutes three times per week.

The last goal is the most useful because it's clear and easy to measure, whereas the first goal isn't measurable and the second is vague. Instead of striving to do more or less of something, quantify *how much* more or less you'll do.

Achievable: Is your goal something that you can realistically accomplish? Is it within your control to achieve it? It's important to set yourself up for success by setting a modest goal. This can mean breaking a large goal into smaller pieces. For example, if you're currently not eating any vegetables, striving to eat five a day probably isn't realistic. Instead, you might start with a goal of eating one serving of vegetables daily and once you've accomplished that for a week, increase your goal to two servings.

You also want to make sure that the desired outcome is something you can control. For example, you might want to have fewer panic attacks, but that outcome isn't completely in your control. Instead, create a goal to do something that will likely lead to that outcome, such as meditating, exercising, or taking medication daily, as these are all within your power and are likely to reduce your panic attacks.

Relevant: Does this goal align with your longer term goals and priorities? Does it seem worth doing? You want to spend your time and energy on goals that matter to you and are likely to improve your life. In the previous exercise, you chose the most relevant issue to focus on by considering the negative effects of certain behaviors and your motivation level.

Time-bound: What is the time line for accomplishing each step of your plan? A realistic schedule can help you make progress because you're more likely to follow through when you've specified when you'll do things.

Time lines are helpful, but end dates or deadlines aren't a good idea if you want to permanently change your behavior. A completion date implies that once you've accomplished your goal, you'll stop doing the new behavior. For example, a goal to exercise every day until my sister's wedding suggests that my daily exercise routine ends after the wedding.

Now create a SMART goal for the behavior that you'd like to manage better.

Behavior to change: _____

Example: Staying up late

Goal: _____

_____

_____

Example: Go to bed at 10 p.m.. I'll go to bed fifteen minutes earlier each week (11:45 this week, 11:30 next week, and so forth until I'm in bed at 10 p.m.). I'll set a bedtime alarm to remind me.

Finally, check that you've included all the components of SMART goals by asking yourself these questions:

- Is my goal specific?

- How will I know whether I've achieved my goal? Can I measure my progress or success?

- Is it something I can realistically achieve?

- Is it important to me?

- When will I make these changes?

If you can improve your goal, go back and adjust it. Personal goals are works in progress, so it's perfectly fine to continue to adjust them. For example, once you start implementing your goal, you may find that it isn't realistic and you need to give yourself more time. Adjusting your goal is preferable to quitting or pushing through and causing yourself more stress. You want to set achievable goals that will improve your life now and in the future.

Step 3: Be Kind to Yourself

Setting limits with yourself takes a lot of effort. It's especially hard to sustain that effort if you're not seeing the progress you'd hoped for. But behavior change isn't all forward progress. It's normal to have setbacks and feel discouraged at times. Self-compassion can help you stick to your goals, even when things get hard.

Most people automatically respond to a setback or mistake with self-criticism. But a harsh inner critic that says, *You're a failure* or *You're lazy* doesn't motivate us to do better. In *The Mindful Self-Compassion Workbook*, Neff and Germer (2018) explain that self-criticism is rooted in fear—fear of becoming an alcoholic like your father, fear of having a heart attack if you don't change your diet, or fear of being fired if you make another mistake. Fear might temporarily motivate you, but it doesn't lead to lasting change. Instead, it makes us feel ashamed, inadequate, and discouraged. And then we're more likely to give up.

Self-compassion, however, is motivating. "Compassion inclines us toward long-term health and well-being, not short-term pleasure...Research shows self-compassionate people engage in healthier behaviors like exercise, eating well, drinking less, and going to the doctor more regularly" (21).

In the next exercise, you'll practice transforming self-criticism into self-compassion because criticism doesn't increase self-discipline or help you reach your goals. Acknowledging that criticism may be a misguided attempt to protect or motivate yourself can make it easier to replace it with self-compassion.

Think of some occasions when you didn't manage your behavior as you wanted. On the following chart, record what you said to yourself, what your fears were, and how you could respond with kindness and understanding, as you might respond to a friend in the same situation. Try to include the three elements of self-compassion in your response: 1) being kind to yourself rather than judgmental or critical, 2) recognizing that everyone struggles and you aren't the only one who has made this mistake, and 3) being aware of your feelings and acknowledging how painful this experience is without overidentifying with it (Neff 2011).

Situation	What did your inner critic say?	How might your inner critic be trying to protect or motivate you? What fears might your inner critic be trying to alert you to?	What can you say to yourself in this situation that is kind and supports your goals?
Example: I got drunk and slept with my ex.	I'm such an idiot.	My inner critic doesn't want me to drink so much because I make bad decisions when I do. My inner critic is afraid that I'll keep going back to Aaron and I'll never have a happy, mature relationship.	It was a mistake to get drunk and sleep with Aaron, but I understand why I did it. I'm having a hard time and wanted comfort. I'm not an idiot, but I do need to break this pattern.

If you'd like to continue practicing this exercise, download the Compassionate Self-Talk chart at http://www.newharbinger.com/47582.

In addition to speaking kindly to yourself, you can demonstrate love and self-acceptance through actions such as taking a hot bath, giving yourself a hug or neck massage, savoring a healthy treat, or whatever feels comforting to you.

When to Seek Help

Many people achieve better results when they get help with their self-management goals. Fortunately, there are numerous ways to get help these days, including professional help from a doctor or therapist, educational classes such as smoking cessation or weight loss programs, peer support groups such as 12-step programs, and app-based habit-tracking tools. Even telling a friend about your goals can provide helpful support and accountability.

SMART goals can help us make behavioral changes, but they don't address deeper unmet needs and emotional wounds that sometimes surface when we try to change our behavior. For example, someone who struggles with alcoholism may have trouble staying sober because they don't know how to tolerate the painful feelings and memories that they experience when they're sober. If your self-management struggles are causing significant problems or are getting worse, you may need professional help. However, many of us don't seek help because we think it will be expensive, time-consuming, embarrassing, or because we feel hopeless. If this is the case for you, use the writing prompts in this section to explore your thoughts and options.

What's preventing you from getting help?

The barriers you're facing may be real or they may be assumptions. Often, we assume that anger management classes will be expensive or that we're not eligible for paid time off to go to treatment, but we don't know for sure. So, do some research, talk to your doctor, call the 2-1-1 information line (available in most of the US), or talk to your health insurer and human resources department. There may be more options than you thought.

However, there may still be sacrifices involved in getting help, so think about what you might gain by getting help and what might happen if you don't.

What might you gain by seeking help?

_____

_____

_____

_____

_____

What do you think will happen if you don't get help?

_____

_____

_____

_____

_____

_____

The bottom line is that seeking help and finding viable options takes perseverance and hard work, but can ultimately help you take control of your life and rebuild your health and relationships.

Summary

Boundaries are an important self-management tool; they foster structure, healthy habits, and the stability we need to keep our lives running smoothly. In this chapter, we reviewed how to use SMART goals to define and structure our efforts toward better self-management. We also discussed the role of self-compassion and seeking help in reaching our goals, especially when we get off-track and feel discouraged. Technology use is another area of self-management where most of us struggle, so the next chapter is devoted to setting boundaries with technology.

Chapter 14

Boundaries with Technology

In a relatively short amount of time, technology has transformed almost every aspect of our lives. Mobile phones and laptop computers, which were supposed to give us newfound freedoms—to work from home, stay informed, and take phone calls anywhere—can now feel like a leash, making it impossible to get away from work, anxiety-producing news, and intrusive friends. And things like texting, online shopping, and on-demand movies are convenient and fun, but they can interfere with our productivity, goals, and relationships, especially if we don't know how to limit our use.

As technology continues to advance, it's increasingly important that we learn how to set boundaries with it, so it doesn't hijack our relationships, health, and emotions. But before we start making rules for managing our technology use, we need to understand how we're using it and how technology is helping and hurting us.

How Technology Helps Us

Technology is such a big part of our lives that we take much of it for granted. We rely on texting for quick replies to our questions, calendar notifications to remind us of appointments, social media to keep us connected to friends and relatives, and so much more. You may use technology to accomplish some of these common tasks:

- Productivity and practical tasks (banking, researching, organizing, shopping)

- Communicating (phone calls, text messages, email, social media)

- Entertainment (television, movies, music, games, shopping, social media)

- Self-care and health (music, telehealth appointments, exercise tracking, meditation apps)

- Learning and staying informed (books, podcasts, online classes, news)

- Creative projects (taking photos, recording and editing videos or music)

How does technology improve your life?

_____

_____

_____

_____

What conveniences of technology would you miss if they didn't exist?

_____

_____

_____

_____

However, as you know, technology can also cause problems.

How Technology Causes Problems

Like a lot of things, technology is an asset when it's used in moderation. But it's so easy to access (everyone has a smartphone in their pocket) and so appealing (nearly limitless content, instant gratification, bright colors and sounds) that we often overuse it. For many of us, it's hard to avoid the temptation of just one more episode of our favorite show or ordering one more thing to be delivered tomorrow.

However, it's not just how much time we spend in front of our devices that causes problems; it's also what we do online. For example, spending eight hours in front of a computer because it's your job probably won't cause as many problems as spending the same amount of time watching movies or playing games.

We need to be mindful of why we're using technology, and whether we're accomplishing our intended goals. Quite often, we pick up our phones intending to do one thing but get distracted and end up wasting time. Or we open a social media app hoping to get a happiness boost from connecting with friends, but we see pictures from a party we weren't invited to or divisive political comments and feel disappointed, frustrated, or anxious—not happier or more relaxed.

Below are some signs your technology use needs better boundaries. We're all different, of course, so you may experience somewhat different effects, but these warning signs are worth keeping in mind:

- You're not meeting deadlines, completing tasks, or fulfilling your responsibilities.

- Your loved ones complain about your use.

- You don't want your children to emulate you.

- You're frequently distracted by technology.

- You often feel worse after spending time on social media, the internet, or your phone.

- Technology interferes with your sleep or worsens other health problems.

- You feel anxious if you can't get online or check your phone.

How does your technology use negatively affect you and those around you?

_____

_____

_____

_____

_____

Knowing whether it's the amount of time, type of activities, or both that are causing problems will help you pinpoint the type of boundaries you need with technology. You may have a sense of where the problem lies, but do some tracking to collect more data; most people underestimate how much time they spend online. Tracking your technology use is a bit cumbersome if you use multiple devices or use them in short bursts. However, most computers and smartphones provide some of this data (check *Screen Time* on Apple devices, *Digital Wellbeing* on Android devices, or use an application such as *Time Sense* on computers running Windows). Record your data on the chart below. Additional copies of this Technology Use Tracker are available at http://www.newharbinger.com/47582.

Time of Day	Total Time Spent	Activity or App	Thoughts or Feelings

Once you've completed tracking, review the data you've collected.

How much total time did you spend using technology today?   _____

What activities or apps did you spend the most time using?

_____

_____

_____

_____

_____

What times of day did you use the most screen time?

_____

_____

_____

_____

_____

What do you think or feel about your use? If you noticed any patterns or areas of concern, what are they?

_____

_____

_____

_____

_____

We spend time online for different purposes and to meet different needs. If you can identify the underlying need that you're trying to meet online, you'll be more successful at setting a boundary and finding an alternative way to meet your need. For example, are you shopping online for a birthday present for your mother? Or are you shopping because you're bored or anxious? Targeted activities like shopping for a birthday present are less likely to lead to problematic technology use than scrolling through websites trying to make yourself feel better.

Identify a specific technology-use problem. What underlying needs are you trying to meet with this activity?

_____

_____

_____

_____

_____

Now that you have a good sense of what aspects of your technology use need better boundaries, you're ready to set them.

Are You Addicted to Technology?   Although the American Psychological Association doesn't recognize technology addiction in the *Diagnostic and Statistical Manual of Mental Disorders*, many mental health professionals believe you can become addicted to the internet, video games, online gambling, and online sex or pornography. Signs of these addictions include:

- Compulsive use (failed efforts to quit or reduce your use, continued use despite negative consequences, thinking about what's happening online when you're not there)

- Tolerance (spending more and more time online)

- Withdrawal symptoms (irritability, restlessness, anxiety, or depression when you can't get online)

You can locate clinicians who specialize in technology addictions in directories such as PsychologyToday.com and GoodTherapy.org. You can also find an internet addiction resource in the Resources list that's available at http://www.newharbinger.com/47582

Setting Boundaries with Technology

Let's focus on two main types of boundaries with technology. The first are limits you set to manage your technology use, which may include time limits, content limits, and location limits. The second are limits for how and when you'll be available to others through technology. This includes things like when you'll respond to after-hours work emails or who can message you on social media.

Limiting Your Own Technology Use

Using the data that you collected by tracking, answer the following questions to establish guidelines to limit your technology use.

What technology will you use? Are there any devices, applications, or websites that you won't use? Which do you need to limit?

_____

_____

_____

_____

_____

When will you use your phone or other devices and when will you refrain from using them?

_____

_____

_____

_____

_____

Where will you use your devices and where will you not use them?

_____

_____

_____

_____

_____

How much time will you spend using technology per day?

_____

_____

_____

_____

_____

What will you do instead? Think about the underlying needs that you're trying to meet with your problematic technology use and consider how else you could meet those needs.

_____

_____

_____

_____

_____

TECH-FREE TIMES AND SPACES

Building on these limits, many individuals and families find it helpful to create tech-free times and spaces. Often, mealtimes and bedrooms are desirable tech-free times and spaces. This helps us eliminate distractions and stressors so we can build relationships, encourage conversation while eating, and relax before bedtime.

Tech-free times and spaces work best when there are strict boundaries (no exceptions) and everyone in the family agrees to abide by them. However, if your partner or someone else in your household won't agree, you can still benefit by choosing to abstain from technology at particular times and locations. And it's possible others will get on board with the idea after observing your behavior.

What tech-free times or spaces would help you or your family prioritize what's most important to you?

_____

_____

_____

_____

_____

MAKE IT INCONVENIENT

You can also use the strategy of inconvenience to break a bad habit, according to Gretchen Rubin (2015). The idea is that the harder it is to do something, the less likely we are to do it. So, to cut back on certain activities, make it harder to do them. Here are some ways to apply this strategy to problem technology use:

- Delete time-wasting or problem-causing apps or hide them in folders that are harder to get to. Sometimes, out of sight is out of mind and you may avoid temptation if they aren't in plain sight.

- To avoid checking your phone, put it in the glove compartment while driving or in another room while working or sleeping.

- Log out of websites when you're done and don't save your username and password, making it more work to access them again.

- Disable one-click shopping and don't store your credit card number on your computer or shopping websites. Instead, make yourself get up and retrieve your card and manually enter the numbers.

- Remove the batteries from the remote control and store them in another room.

- Block websites that you overuse.

- Don't subscribe to every streaming service. Limiting your choices can help you limit your use.

- Purchase a smaller data plan. Knowing you'll have to pay overage charges may encourage less use.

Some of these ideas may seem silly and inconsequential, but they can be just enough of an annoyance or inconvenience that you think twice about engaging with technology. Often, we just need to keep ourselves from doing it for a short time, until the urge passes or we get involved in another activity.

How will you try to limit technology use by making it inconvenient?

_____

_____

_____

_____

_____

Limiting How Others Interact with You Online

Technology not only allows us to be available to virtually anyone at any time, but it's also become the expectation. However, that doesn't mean we *should* make ourselves accessible 24/7. Letting friends text you at all hours, your boss call you on weekends, or your abusive ex-partner direct message you on social media isn't good for you. You need boundaries in these situations to protect your physical and emotional health, privacy, time, and relationships.

Boundaries are built on personal rights. So, let's review your rights related to technology. You have the right to:

- Turn off your phone.

- Not answer calls, emails, or text messages.

- End a phone call.

- Leave a group message.

- Set a time limit for a call.

- Block people from contacting you.

- Be treated with respect.

- Keep your passwords and accounts private.

- Unfollow or unfriend people on social media.

- Take any of the above actions without explaining or justifying them to people who repeatedly violate your boundaries, threaten you, or hurt you.

Again, guilt can be a big obstacle to setting boundaries, which is why it's so important to know your rights and that you cannot and should not make yourself available to everyone all the time. It's healthy to set boundaries to protect yourself and meet your other needs.

How has being too accessible or available negatively affected you or your family?

_____

_____

_____

_____

_____

What boundaries do you need to set to limit your accessibility? Consider who, what platforms or methods of communication, and times you need to limit.

_____

_____

_____

_____

If you need to set boundaries in a professional or close personal relationship, you may want to communicate your boundary, especially if it's a change from your previous behavior, so others know what to expect from you. For example, you might tell your coworkers, *I check my messages for the last time at 7 p.m. I'll respond to anything that comes in after that in the morning.* Or you might tell a friend who gets anxious if you don't respond to her text messages immediately that you're not ignoring her, but trying to limit how much time you spend on your phone and will usually get back to her within two hours.

Use Technology to Your Advantage

Ironically, technology gives us some helpful tools for setting boundaries with technology. However, technology changes so quickly that by the time you're reading this, some may be outdated and new ones may be available. Here are some ideas to get you started:

- Turn off notifications to avoid distractions.

- Use an email autoresponder so you don't have to reply to messages when you're on vacation or during nonwork hours.

- Set an alarm to remind you when you've used your quota of screen time.

- Use the *Do Not Disturb* setting to prevent being disturbed by particular people or at certain times of day.

- Block people on your phone, email, or social media accounts to keep them from contacting you.

- Password protect your electronic devices to maintain your privacy.

- Limit who can contact you or view your profile on social media platforms.

- Unfollow or unfriend people on social media who make you feel bad.

- Change your phone to grayscale to make it less enticing.

- Use *Bedtime* or *Sleep Mode* to avoid disruptions during specified sleep hours.

- Use *Screen Time* (Apple devices) or *Digital Wellbeing* (Android devices) to limit how much time you spend on particular apps and websites, pause notifications, prevent you from downloading apps, and switch off work apps and notifications during nonwork hours.

Frankly, the number of tools, settings, and applications available for managing your screen time can be overwhelming. You may need to experiment with different settings and options until you find the right combination to support your goals. You may also need to ask someone who's more technologically savvy to help you navigate your options.

What tools or applications will you use to manage your screen time? Or who can help you?

_____

_____

_____

_____

_____

For parents, limiting children's screen time and teaching them to set boundaries with technology is a big job. Although these topics are beyond the scope of this book, you can use many of the settings and tools listed above to limit your children's technology use as well.

Summary

You now have a better understanding of how technology causes problems for you and you have tools to help you limit your use. However, since technology is such a big part of our lives and it changes quickly, setting boundaries with technology will be an ongoing effort. Continuing to monitor your use will help you stay ahead of problems before they become too big.

You've now completed all the boundary skills in this workbook! In the conclusion, we'll review the most important concepts and skills and I'll give you some tips for staying motivated and trouble-shooting problems that may arise as you continue to practice your boundary skills.

Conclusion

As you finish this workbook, you're well on your way to setting better boundaries! Learning new skills is a process and it's normal to have setbacks and feel discouraged at times. So, we'll wrap up this book by reviewing some important concepts and ways to stay motivated.

Important Concepts

We've covered a lot of concepts in this book and hopefully many were impactful. You may have even had a few aha moments when you understood an idea in a new way or had a meaningful insight. To reinforce the concepts that resonated with you, skim the chapters and jot down those that stood out and how they were helpful.

	Important concepts	How have these concepts helped you?
Chapter 1		
Chapter 2		
Chapter 3		
Chapter 4		
Chapter 5		
Chapter 6		
Chapter 7		

Chapter 8		
Chapter 9		
Chapter 10		
Chapter 11		
Chapter 12		
Chapter 13		
Chapter 14		

Because learning is ongoing, it can also be helpful to revisit the concepts and exercises that challenged you. Which concepts or exercises might you benefit from revisiting?

_____

_____

_____

_____

_____

Stay Motivated

As you know, setting boundaries is hard work. You may feel discouraged or unmotivated sometimes, especially when you make mistakes and encounter setbacks. The following tips can help you stay motivated.

LEARN FROM MISTAKES

It doesn't feel good to make mistakes, so we usually try to avoid them. But mistakes are a normal part of the learning process—and can even be helpful. Try to reframe one of your recent boundary-setting mistakes as a learning opportunity. The following questions can help.

What did you learn from this experience?

_____

_____

_____

_____

_____

What will you do differently next time?

_____

_____

_____

_____

_____

What skills do you need to practice further?

_____

_____

_____

_____

_____

What went well in this attempt to set a boundary?

_____

_____

_____

_____

_____

BE KIND TO YOURSELF

We also need to watch that frustration and disappointment don't lead to self-criticism, which is demotivating and makes it harder to set boundaries because it reinforces negative beliefs about ourselves. Offering yourself kindness is more productive and will lead to better results in the future. One way to do this is by saying something compassionate and reassuring to yourself, such as:

- This is hard, but I'll try again.

- I'll succeed if I keep at it.

- Everyone makes mistakes and does things imperfectly.

- The more I practice, the easier this will get.

- I'm choosing to confront my fears.

- It's normal to feel uncomfortable and afraid when setting new boundaries.

- Uncomfortable feelings will pass.

- I have the right to be treated with dignity and respect.

If you feel discouraged, what compassionate words can you offer yourself?

_____

_____

_____

_____

_____

NOTICE YOUR SUCCESSES

Another way to stay motivated and build confidence is to intentionally draw attention to your successes and progress.

List some of your boundary-setting successes below. Remember, you're looking for progress, not perfection. Small steps add up to big changes!

_____

_____

_____

_____

_____

It's also helpful to keep a list of successes on your phone or in a notebook by your bed, so you can easily add to it and review it periodically for encouragement.

Final Thoughts

Completing this workbook is an amazing accomplishment and I'm sure you've benefited from the hard work you've put in. Of course, your journey to better boundaries doesn't end here! As I've said throughout this book, setting boundaries is an ongoing process that needs practice and adjusting as your needs, goals, and relationships change. So, I encourage you to continue practicing the boundary skills in this book, honoring your needs, and treating yourself with kindness and respect. With this as your foundation, your boundaries, self-esteem, and relationships will flourish.

Acknowledgments

No one writes a book alone! I want to extend a big thank you to those who've supported me and this project.

Thank you to…

Ryan Buresh, for helping flesh out the idea for this book and making it a reality.

The editors and staff at New Harbinger Publications, for their professionalism, attention to detail, and commitment to mental health.

Michelle Farris, for being my sounding board and cheerleader.

My family, for their flexibility and support.

And my readers, clients, and colleagues, for their inspiration and encouragement.

Appendix

Universal Human Needs

- Physical safety
- Emotional safety
- Respect
- Appreciation
- Love
- Acceptance
- Understanding
- Trust
- Honesty
- Kindness
- Help or support
- Physical touch
- Connection
- Privacy or to be alone
- Fun
- Quiet
- Excitement or novelty
- Creative outlets
- To be challenged
- Food and water
- Rest and sleep
- Independence or autonomy
- Spiritual connection

Four Steps to Setting Better Boundaries

Step 1: Clarify What You Need and Want

- What is my boundary-related problem?

- What are my unmet needs in this situation?

- How do I feel in this situation? How do I want to feel?

- What outcome do I want? What do I want to accomplish by setting a boundary?

- I need _____ and want to feel_____ when _____.

Step 2: Identify Your Boundaries

- What are my options?

- Which of these options is within my control?

- Which option makes the most sense for me?

Step 3: Implement Your Boundaries

- What actions will I take? What will I say? When and where will I take these actions?

- What action or change, if any, do I need to request from someone else?

- What will I do if they resist, ignore, or respond with anger to my boundary?

- How will I know if this boundary is working?

- What obstacles might I encounter? How will I handle them?

Step 4: Fine-Tune Your Boundaries

- Was my boundary successful? Were my needs met? Did it create the positive feelings I wanted?

- Did I experience any of the boundary pitfalls (not following through, misidentifying my needs or feelings, not getting cooperation, giving up too soon)?

- What adjustment do I need to make?

References

Breitman, Patti, and Connie Hatch. 2001. *How to Say No Without Feeling Guilty*. New York: Broadway Books.

Brown, Brené. 2015. *Rising Strong*. New York: Spiegel & Grau.

Hanks, Julie de Azevedo. 2016. *The Assertiveness Guide for Women*. Oakland, CA: New Harbinger Publications.

Lewicki, Roy J., B. Polin, and R. B. Lount Jr. 2016. "An Exploration of the Structure of Effective Apologies." *Negotiation and Conflict Management Research* 9: 177–196.

Martin, Sharon. 2019. *The CBT Workbook for Perfectionism*. Oakland, CA: New Harbinger Publications.

Neff, Kristin. 2011. *Self-Compassion: The Proven Power of Being Kind to Yourself*. New York: William Morrow.

Neff, Kristin, and Christopher Germer. 2018. *The Mindful Self-Compassion Workbook*. New York: Guilford Press.

Palmer, Vicki Tidwell. 2016. *Moving Beyond Betrayal: The 5-Step Boundary Solution for Partners of Sex Addicts*. Las Vegas: Central Recovery Press.

Real, Terence. 2008. *The New Rules of Marriage*. New York: Ballantine Books.

Rosenberg, Marshall B. 2003. *Nonviolent Communication: A Language of Life*. Encinitas, CA: PuddleDancer Press.

Rubin, Gretchen. 2015. *Better Than Before: What I Learned About Making and Breaking Habits—to Sleep More, Quit Sugar, Procrastinate Less, and Generally Build a Happier Life*. New York: Broadway Books.

Sharon Martin, MSW, LCSW, is a licensed psychotherapist in San Jose, CA, specializing in helping individuals struggling with perfectionism, codependency, and people-pleasing using cognitive behavioral therapy (CBT), mindfulness, and self-compassion. Martin is author of *The CBT Workbook for Perfectionism*, writes the *Conquering Codependency* blog for *Psychology Today*, and is a regular media contributor on emotional health and relationships.

Real Change *Is* Possible

For more than forty-five years, New Harbinger has published proven-effective self-help books and pioneering workbooks to help readers of all ages and backgrounds improve mental health and well-being, and achieve lasting personal growth. In addition, our spirituality books offer profound guidance for deepening awareness and cultivating healing, self-discovery, and fulfillment.

Founded by psychologist Matthew McKay and Patrick Fanning, New Harbinger is proud to be an independent, employee-owned company. Our books reflect our core values of integrity, innovation, commitment, sustainability, compassion, and trust. Written by leaders in the field and recommended by therapists worldwide, New Harbinger books are practical, accessible, and provide real tools for real change.

 **newharbinger**publications

MORE BOOKS from
NEW HARBINGER PUBLICATIONS

ADULT CHILDREN OF EMOTIONALLY IMMATURE PARENTS

How to Heal from Distant, Rejecting, or Self-Involved Parents

978-1626251700 / US $18.95

THE HIGHLY SENSITIVE PERSON'S GUIDE TO DEALING WITH TOXIC PEOPLE

How to Reclaim Your Power from Narcissists and Other Manipulators

978-1684035304 / US $16.95

DISARMING THE NARCISSIST, THIRD EDITION

Surviving and Thriving with the Self-Absorbed

978-1684037704 / US $17.95

PERFECTLY HIDDEN DEPRESSION

How to Break Free from the Perfectionism That Masks Your Depression

978-1684033584 / US $16.95

MESSAGES, FOURTH EDITION

The Communication Skills Book

978-1684031719 / US $21.95

THE STRESS-PROOF BRAIN

Master Your Emotional Response to Stress Using Mindfulness and Neuroplasticity

978-1626252660 / US $17.95

Did you know there are free tools you can download for this book?

Free tools are things like **worksheets, guided meditation exercises**, and **more** that will help you get the most out of your book.

You can download free tools for this book—whether you bought or borrowed it, in any format, from any source— from the **New Harbinger** website. All you need is a NewHarbinger.com account. Just use the URL provided in this book to view the free tools that are available for it. Then, click on the "download" button for the free tool you want, and follow the prompts that appear to log in to your NewHarbinger.com account and download the material.

You can also save the free tools for this book to your **Free Tools Library** so you can access them again anytime, just by logging in to your account! Just look for this button on the book's free tools page:

+ save this to my
free tools library

If you need help accessing or downloading free tools, visit **newharbinger.com/faq** or contact us at customerservice@newharbinger.com.

CELEBRATING
40 YEARS